the luxury of dual shower control

GATE VALVES

Designed for economy and efficiency. Sizes

Minimum wear, maximum reliability.

Spec... Hospital Supp...

Engine Test Benches

LEONA...

WALKER

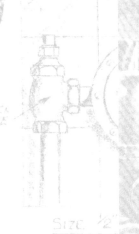

In pursuit of showering perfection

The story of Kohler Mira

In pursuit of showering perfection

The story of Kohler Mira

Nigel Watson

First published in 2022 in Great Britain
on behalf of Kohler Mira Ltd by
St Matthew's Press
10, St Matthew's Terrace, Leyburn
North Yorkshire DL8 5EL
www.corporatehistories.org.uk

Kohler Mira Ltd
Cromwell Road
Cheltenham
Gloucestershire GL52 5EP
Tel: 0800 001 4040
Email: askus@mirashowers.com
Copyright © Nigel Watson and Kohler Mira Ltd

ISBN 978-1-8383994-7-4

Design and artwork by Matthew Wilson: Editorial + Publishing Design
www.mexington.co.uk
Printed and bound by Pureprint Group
Bellbrook Park, Uckfield, East Sussex TN22 1PL

Contents

Foreword

To mark the 100th anniversary of Kohler Mira Ltd, I thought it would be nice to delve into the archives to tell the story of this amazing business that I have been lucky to be part of for a quarter of its century.

As we started to work with Nigel Watson and uncovered more and more of the back story, it struck me that while so much has changed, equally many things remain the same. Not least our dedication to the pursuit of showering perfection and the meticulous detail that goes into our products in order to ensure we give our customers the best possible experience. It is also our ethos of innovation that has ensured that, from the introduction of the first ever thermostatic shower to our most recent digital showering technology, we have always led the way. It is this, coupled with the passion of our associates, that sets us apart and has done so throughout our history.

Since our founding in 1921, we have lived through the reigns of four monarchs and the leadership of nearly 20 prime ministers. We have withstood economic depression, two world wars and most recently a global pandemic. How? Through the passion, commitment and drive of our associates and the quality and reliability of our products and services.

I would like to take this opportunity to thank every single one of our employees past and present for the contribution they made and in particular those who contributed to the writing of this book. It is my honour and privilege to be leading this business during our special centenary year.

Craig Baker
Managing Director

1

Beginnings: 1921–37

When Walter Crosweller and James Walker founded Walker Crosweller, the predecessor of Kohler Mira, in March 1921, it was not to sell showers. Showers were almost completely unknown in British households since few of them had a separate bathroom. The adoption of a facility everyone today takes for granted was slow. Just under half of British homes lacked a bathroom in 1947, and 20 years later they were still absent from a quarter of households. While today nearly 90 per cent of UK houses have at least one shower, in 1921 they were largely seen only in public or semi-public settings such as public baths, changing rooms, boarding schools, hospitals and sanitoria. It was only in the 1960s that they became more popular as the country became more prosperous; the state encouraged their installation in new houses and offered grants for their installation in older properties. Walker Crosweller played its part, claiming that its mass media campaign, which promoted the first Mira showers, effectively created the domestic shower market. Today Kohler Mira is the UK's leading domestic shower company.

Walker Crosweller was set up to sell imported steam traps, continuing a business Walter

Crosweller had been part of since before the First World War. It was the thermostatic aspect of these devices, used to filter out condensate and conserve steam in industrial applications, that eventually led the business to concentrate on making and selling thermostatic mixing valves, which would in turn lead to the first Mira showers.

Although the new business struggled during the tough economic climate of the 1920s, its ultimate success was founded on the complementary skills of its two founders. While Walter Crosweller was the inventive engineer and James Walker the enthusiastic salesman, each of them understood the other's aptitude. Selling had been a key part of Walter Crosweller's engineering role, while technical knowledge was central to James Walker's career in advertising. Thus, when Walker Crosweller began manufacturing for the first time, the business was sales-driven rather than production-led, a crucial factor in its progress.

Another characteristic of the business from the outset was the consideration it had for its employees. The first employee was a Miss Ellis, 'our one and only assistant', Walter Crosweller later recalled. By 1925, Miss Ellis had been joined by Miss Helmes, Miss Daly, Miss Hall, Miss Batten,

No. 232115

Certificate of Incorporation

I Hereby Certify, That

WALKER, CROSWELLER & COMPANY, LIMITED

is this day Incorporated under the Companies Act, 1929, and that the Company is Limited.

Given under my hand at London this   twentieth   day of   November   One Thousand Nine Hundred and   thirty .

Registrar of Companies.

Certificate received by :   Date   25 Nov 1930

The Founders: Walter Crosweller (1888–1950) and James Walker (1879–1963)

Walter Crosweller was born in Highbury, London, the son of a painter and decorator. After leaving elementary school at the age of 13, he won a scholarship to study at the East London Technical College. Established in 1896, and later part of Queen Mary College, it was one of the new educational institutions intended to help the country catch up with the technical progress made by its rivals, particularly Germany.

In 1904, Walter won an apprenticeship with Poplar shipbuilders Yarrow & Co., and continued his studies in mechanical engineering part-time at the college and Hackney Evening Institute for the next eight years. By then, he was working as an engineer for Sanders, Rehders & Co. Ltd, the forerunners of Spirax-Sarco, which he joined in 1911. The business had been set up in 1888 to import thermostatic steam traps from Germany, sold under the Sarco brand name.

Within months of joining, still only 22, he was sent to take charge of the company's recently opened New York office. He must have returned before the First World War, which seriously weakened the UK business since it relied on the sale of products imported mainly from Germany. His entry in the records of the Institution of

James Macfarlane Walker (1879–1963), co-founder with Walter Crosweller of Walker Crosweller.

Mechanical Engineers for 1919 shows that he was working on the commercial application of mechanical steam raising and already had patents in his name.

In 1921 Walter left the failing business shortly before it collapsed to set up Walker, Crosweller & Co. in partnership with James Walker.

James Walker was born in Inverkeithing in Fife. His father worked in the iron trade, later moving to Manchester as a foundry manager. James won a scholarship to Manchester Grammar School, leaving to study at Salford Technical College, where he gained the knowledge that he later applied effectively in his partnership with Walter Crosweller. But his real love was selling. After some years as a commercial traveller, by 1911 he was advertising manager for *The Manchester Guardian*. It was at his suggestion that the newspaper first carried an engineering page, for which he sold space.

The two men must have met in Manchester when Walter Crosweller was manager of the northern office of Sanders, Rehders & Co. After the war, they renewed their friendship in London, where James Walker was running his own advertising agency and Walter Crosweller was back in the company's head office.

The first of a series of staff letters, highlighting flexible working arrangements.

WALKER, CROSWELLER
& COMPANY
DANE'S INN HOUSE
265 STRAND
LONDON, W.C.2

INDICATING & RECORDING
INSTRUMENTS
For BOILER HOUSE & WORKS CONTROL

TELEPHONE: CENTRAL 1963
TELEGRAMS: "INSTRUKEMI
ESTRAND, LONDON"
CABLES: "INSTRUKEMI, LONDON"
CODES: BENTLEY'S; WESTERN
UNION; ABC, 5th EDITION

CO₂ RECORDERS
O₂, SO₂ and CI RECORDERS
GAS DENSITY RECORDERS

HIGH VACUUM RECORDERS
DRAUGHT AND PRESSURE GAUGES
DIFFERENTIAL AND REVERSION RECORDERS

THERMOMETERS
ELECTRICAL PYROMETERS
GAS VOLUME RECORDERS

16th June 1925.

STAFF LETTER NO. 1.

It has been decided to give each member of the Staff one Saturday morning off each calendar month until further notice.

The order of leave will be as set out below and as this has been arranged to fit in best with each person's duties no changing or exchanging of dates will be allowed.

First Saturday in the month Miss Helmes & Daly.
Second " " " " " Ellis & Hall.
Third " " " " Mr Connor & Miss Batten.
Fourth " " " " " Burton & Tinniswood.

WALKER, CROSWELLER & CO.,

C/E-A

Mr Burton, Mr Connor and Mr Tinniswood. When it was common for people to work six days a week – the weekend as we know it was gradually adopted by UK businesses between the wars – Walker Crosweller gave employees one Saturday morning off every month. There were conditions to this concession; it was suspended during busy times (for example, when the business was preparing for trade exhibitions), and it was withdrawn from staff who had been more than 60 minutes late for work in any preceding month.

When the partners opened their office in a single room in Danes Inn House on the Strand in London in 1921, they capitalised on their previous experience and reached an agreement with the Steam Fittings Company, later renamed Drayton

The firm's staff in 1926 (left to right) Miss Howe, Miss Ellis, Miss Helmes, Miss Bottomley, Messrs Daly, Hall and Milford. (Courtesy of Spirax-Sarco Engineering plc.)

Regulator & Instrument Company, for the sale of their range of Arkon steam traps and instrument regulators. Two years later, Walter Crosweller was contacted by his former employer, Clement Wells. He had recruited Crosweller to Sanders, Rehders in 1911 and was running Sarco Co. Inc., which had taken over the US business. Sarco wanted to export its thermostatic steam traps to the UK, and Wells invited Walker Crosweller to act as the company's agents. At the time, the partners had to decline because of their arrangement with Drayton, but when this expired two years later they took up the offer. Since the Sarco brand in the UK was owned by another company that had emerged out of the collapse of Sanders, Rehders, the US-made traps were given a new name, 'Spirax', taken from the spiral element in the traps. The first consignment arrived on 1 October 1926; sales exceeded a thousand units in 1927 and more than two thousand in 1930. The firm's

office staff rose from 8 in 1925 to 29 in 1930. With the superior Spirax trap, Walter Crosweller later recorded, the business had 'at last found a saleable line of almost universal demand'. The partnership was also the agent for several other companies, which supplied temperature regulators and other industrial measuring instruments.

The renewed relationship with Clement Wells started Walker Crosweller's gradual transition from sales agency to manufacturer. In 1929 the business took on more men to assemble elements imported from the US into bodies cast and machined by external suppliers in the UK. This made more urgent a move to larger premises. These were on the south side of the Thames, a few minutes from Tower Bridge, in Queen Elizabeth Street, on the top floor of a building housing a printing firm, reached by climbing 60 stairs, since the lift was just for goods. The lift

Telephone : Hop 5786 & 2613   Telegrams : Instrukemi, Boroh, London   Cables : Instrukemi, London   Code : Bentley's

WALKER, CROSWELLER
AND COMPANY
Partners : J. M. WALKER & W. W. CROSWELLER, M.I.Mech.E.
54-58 QUEEN ELIZABETH STREET
LONDON, S.E. 1

FOXBORO
INSTRUMENTS

CO₂ and O₂ RECORDERS	GAS VOLUME RECORDERS	THERMOMETERS
SO₂ and Cl₂ RECORDERS	UNIVERSAL PLANIMETERS	TEMPERATURE RECORDERS
SPIRAX STEAM TRAPS	PRESSURE RECORDERS	AUTOMATIC CONTROLLERS
STEAM, WATER & OIL METERS	GAUGES OF ALL KINDS	ELLISON INCLINED GAUGES

27th May, 1929.

STAFF LETTER No. 7.

The Schedule of Saturday morning leave is again
revised and set out below.

No changes of dates can be made except by the
Company.

No leave has been arranged for fifth Saturdays
when these occur in any month.   Saturdays which clash with
Saturdays allowed in holidays cannot be made up by additional
leave :-

First Saturday in each month - Mr. Davies, Miss Foy,
                                W. Lyons and G. Piper.

Second   "   "   "   "   - Mr. Batten, Miss Helmes,
                                J. Daly, Miss Allen & W. Milford.

Third   "   "   "   "   - Mr. Connor, Miss Lockey,
                                W. Payn, Miss Tucker & R. Mann.

Fourth   "   "   "   "   - Mr. Disher, Miss Howe, R. Hall,
                                Miss Bottomley and H. Desmond.

WALKER, CROSWELLER & Co.

The Spirax Manufacturing Company

The new factory was housed in a building at The Cut, 25 Short Street, close to Waterloo Station and a couple of miles away from Queen Elizabeth Street. The first employees were Jack Smith and Harry Green, who began by cleaning the windows and whitewashing the walls. The only equipment comprised a 100-pound gas boiler, a capstan lathe, a vacuum pump and several assembly benches. Herbert Smith's assistant, Stanley Haines, shared an office with him but had no desk of his own. He bought a couple of second-hand wooden three-drawer filing cabinets as pedestals and added a top made from floorboards covered in heavy brown linoleum. The desk was put together by the maintenance man, Oscar, a gentle giant with a wooden leg, and it was still in use at the Cheltenham works in the 1950s.

created an unwelcome draught; the only heating on the floor came from three coke stoves; and the din of printing machinery on the ground floor could be heard all day long. Testing of the steam traps was done on the office kettle.

On 20 November 1930 the business was incorporated as Walker, Crosweller & Co. Ltd. While this reflected the company's growth, it was also a defensive measure to limit the partners' liability as the country began to feel the impact of the great economic depression sweeping the world.

By May 1931, Walter Crosweller was telling staff that 'owing to the prolonged crisis in the business world, certain measures of retrenchment are now unavoidable'. Businesses across the country were cutting pay by 10 per cent, and Walker Crosweller followed suit, exempting only those earning less than thirty shillings a week. 'We believe it will lead to the strengthening of our business and, therefore, the safeguarding of your position.'[1] But the crisis worsened. Sterling was devalued, making goods imported from the US almost a third more expensive. Sarco's steam traps became uncompetitive in a shrinking market, and the government imposed import tariffs of 10 per cent on most goods from countries outside Britain's colonies and dominions. Sales began to evaporate. As one sales representative later recalled, 'We used to call ourselves forgotten men: forgotten in the buyer's waiting room; forgotten by the Chief Engineer, who two hours ago had said he would be down in a minute.'[2]

---

1 Staff Letter No. 15, 22 May 1931.
2 Leonard News, June 1945.

The company's plight was becoming acute. Walter Crosweller was frank with staff. During the autumn of 1931, 'the business on which we all depend was nearly annihilated'. With accumulating losses, it was, he said, 'a very bad time'.[3] Urgent action was needed. The initiative came from Clement Wells, who decided it was time to start making Spirax traps in the UK. A new company, the Spirax Manufacturing Company, was formed in January 1932 as a joint venture between Clement Wells, who held 51 per cent, and Walter Crosweller and James Walker.

Under Herbert Smith, a talented engineer sent over from the US, the first traps were made within three months, with the company sourcing various parts, including the helical tubing, from other suppliers. The first issue of *Spirax News*, published by Walker Crosweller in May 1932, announced that 'our new London Factory is in working order and … production of the 'All British' Spirax Steam Trap has commenced … Every trap without exception is thoroughly tested under working conditions to its full pressure with live steam.'

Sales were boosted by the appointment of an inspirational sales manager, Lionel Northcroft. By October 1932, Walker Crosweller was selling more than a thousand traps every month and the company was able to employ ten representatives selling only traps where previously to make a living they had to sell other lines as well. Sales were divided between a Spirax department and an instruments and general department. 'In less than two years,' wrote Walter Crosweller, 'we have changed over from importers to manufacturers and built up a new sales force.'[4] Northcroft would later write how a crucial part of boosting sales was promoting the technology of steam trapping rather than selling traps as just another item of ironmongery. It was an approach Walker Crosweller would apply with success to later products.

In October 1932, another staff circular was issued under Walter Crosweller's name, addressed 'To my colleagues'.

To reflect that we have got through (as we hope we have) with very few reductions in staff and with only a 10 per cent cut in wages and salaries is very creditable. It reflects credit on the staff for their fine work about the ship and possibly management may take a little credit for some work at the helm.[5]

The company returned to profit during 1932–33 and dividends were waived so a bonus equal to two weeks' salary could be paid to all staff who had been with the business throughout the year. As better times returned, better conditions

3 Staff Letter No. 18, 7 Oct 1932.

4 Staff Letter, August 1933.
5 Ibid., No. 18, 7 Oct 1932.

were introduced. Staff bonuses were standardised according to length of service, and long service was recognised by an extra pound for every year over five years. A specific bonus for long service was introduced for 'greybeards'; six employees were eligible – the longest-serving, Mr Connor, had started work at the firm in January 1922. By the following year, 13 employees were eligible, making up almost half the office staff. Exceptional trading generated special bonuses of one week's salary at Christmas. Staff were encouraged to pay into the National Savings scheme.

The working week became shorter. Half an hour was taken from the working day in April 1933, finishing at 5.30 p.m. rather than 6 p.m., and from the end of the year work on Saturday mornings stopped at 12.30 p.m. rather than 1 p.m. The staff canteen offered sandwiches free of charge from 1934 and hot meals were introduced for a small charge in 1935. (Liver, bacon, sausage or fish were twopence a portion, and vegetables a penny a portion.)

For employees on low salaries, the company offered to pay for all eye tests and dental treatment not covered by the national health insurance scheme. In a city where smog often blotted out the health-giving rays of the sun, Walker Crosweller provided every employee, including those working on the shopfloor of the new instrument-making subsidiary, 'a dose of Radio-Malt in the morning and again in the afternoon'. (Radio-Malt was a malt-

extract containing vitamin D, the 'sunshine' vitamin. It was later replaced by a less sticky alternative, Adexolin, which also contained vitamin A.)

The instrument-making subsidiary was the Arkon Manufacturing Company Ltd, formed in 1933 after Walker Crosweller had acquired the Arkon brand. Making gas and air flow measuring instruments, pressure and vacuum recorders, it struggled for a while, but it provided a platform for a major expansion of manufacturing a few years later. For the time being, the company's revival was driven by the success of Spirax traps. In 1934 the company celebrated a record trading year, sending £100 to Herbert Smith in recognition of the contribution made by the Spirax Manufacturing Company, 'and, thus, in turn to your coming amongst us, starting up the Factory and still remaining closely in charge of its activities'.[6] In the same year, Walter Crosweller could say that 'we have now reached the point where [Sarco Co. Inc.] can sit up and take notice'.[7]

Relations between the joint venture partners were not entirely harmonious despite the long association between Clement Wells and Walter Crosweller. Wells found it frustrating that distance prevented him from having a greater impact on the business, even though he had Herbert Smith as his man on the ground. He came to believe

6   Letter to Herbert Smith, 19 June 1934.

7   The Story of the Firm – speech given by Walter Crosweller in 1934.

Arkon Liquid Meters
meter oil, water, etc.
– first step in control

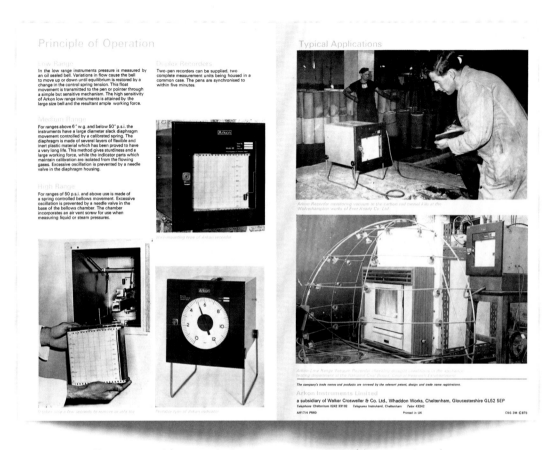

For many years, Arkon measuring instruments were a core part of the company's products.

that Walker and Crosweller were dragging their feet in developing the Spirax business. Making only infrequent visits across the Atlantic, Wells instead kept up a flurry of correspondence. Walter Crosweller and James Walker found the royalty basis of the sales agreement with Sarco irksome. In addition, they were keen to develop other parts of their own business to reduce their reliance on Spirax.

In 1935 an event took place at a psychiatric hospital in Surrey which had far-reaching implications for Walker Crosweller. Dickie Bryant, who was selling Spirax traps, was shown a hospital treatment involving a water bath maintained at a constant pressure, using American-made mixing valves. He was so impressed with the demonstration that he went back to Walker Crosweller and persuaded James Walker and Walter Crosweller to consider adding mixing valves to their product range.

The outcome was that in January 1937 James Walker, accompanied by Lionel Northcroft, sailed across the rough Atlantic seas to finalise an agreement with the innovative entrepreneur who had invented the bimetallic mixing valve witnessed by Dickie Bryant. Frederick C Leonard, the founder

The Leonard Valve Company

Frederick C Leonard arrived in Providence, Rhode Island, from the American Midwest in the early 1900s. He had a technical aptitude, having trained as a watchmaker and qualified as an electrician. When he was scalded in his local barbershop while having a hot shave, he turned his mind towards inventing something that would make hot water safer to use. In 1912 he produced a thermostatic mixing valve, utilising a bimetallic coil as a thermostat to regulate the temperature of the hot and cold water flowing through the valve. The technology has remained largely unchanged to this day. He targeted his invention with considerable success at institutions where fixed baths and showers were commonly used unlike all but the most affluent private households. The Leonard Thermostat Mixing Valve Company was incorporated in 1913 and moved to its present location in Cranston, Rhode Island, in 1930. At the time of James Walker's visit in 1936, the company was known as the Leonard Rooke Company.

of the Leonard Valve Company, came from the same generation as James Walker, and the two men concluded a licence permitting Walker Crosweller to not only manufacture Leonard valves in the UK but also sell them worldwide, excepting the USA, Central and South America. Moreover, unlike the arrangement with Sarco Co. Inc., this was a royalty-free agreement. Seven months later, the first UK-produced Leonard mixing valve was assembled in Walker Crosweller's Queen Elizabeth Street workshop in London. There was excitement at the prospect, with the company magazine announcing in April 1937 how 'the Leonard snowball is beginning to grow'.[8] The pace of activity prompted the company to recruit for the first time a qualified chartered accountant, C H Price, from its auditors, to take charge of the counting house, as the finance department was called.

The opportunity for Walker Crosweller to reduce its reliance on Spirax steam traps and make the Leonard valve the centre of its product range cannot have gone down well with Clement Wells. But Walker Crosweller had also decided the moment had come to go one step further on its manufacturing journey. It was time to move out of the cramped and shabby premises occupied by Walker Crosweller, Arkon and Spirax – news that must have cheered Wells.

The two decisions were made in tandem. The Leonard valve agreement forced the company's

8   Leonard News, April 1937.

The frontage of the company's Art Deco head office with an aerial view of the Cheltenham factory (**below**) shortly after completion in 1937.

hand. 'The advent of Leonard settled the fate of our Queen Elizabeth premises. We could import Leonards there but not make them. Some of us would have said that even Leonard assembly could never have been squeezed into that pint pot, but our excellent works manager, Mr John Eaton, settled that by making a few folks

lift their feet one at a time.'[9] And during 1936, as discussions about the Leonard valve were underway, the company realised that the leases on its London properties were running out. Was London the best place for the company's future? It was almost inevitable that it would have to move out of overcrowded central London, no longer the location for an expanding engineering business. But where to? The suburbs? Or further afield?

Two threads entwined. Firstly, the company looked into the political future and found it uncertain. There was already talk of war

9   Ibid., October 1937.

The Cheltenham factory under construction in 1937. The foreman is in bowler hat and waistcoat. The workmen wear not hard hats but flat caps.

as the government pressed ahead with its rearmament programme. With the threat of aerial bombardment, the capital and its suburbs seemed most at risk and the government was encouraging industry to move out. But other major industrial cities were just as much in jeopardy.

Secondly, towns and cities usually unscathed by economic downturns had been left so scarred by the Depression that they were actively promoting their local economies. One of these was the elegant spa town of Cheltenham in Gloucestershire. The town relied heavily on retired people, whose pensions had dropped after the devaluation of sterling. The population had been falling for some years and many large town houses were unoccupied and up for sale. This earned the town the unfortunate moniker of 'the town to let'. The borough council and the town's chamber of commerce were allies in promoting the town's virtues as a centre for light industry. Posters were distributed all over London proclaiming 'Factory Sites! Why not Cheltenham?'

Perhaps one of these proclamations came to James Walker's attention and prompted him to spend part of his Christmas break in 1936 in

Cheltenham. His walk around the town on Boxing Day was said to have been decisive in persuading him that Cheltenham should be Walker Crosweller's new home.

The company turned down the first site offered to them by the council but accepted a site on the Whaddon Farm estate, which the council had recently acquired. The plan was to build council housing around the factory site in the hope that this would provide most of its labour. Over the years many people from the local neighbourhood have spent their working lives with the company.

The council approved the sale of the three-acre site to the company in April 1937. A few months later, Walker Crosweller paid £2,750 for an additional four and a half acres adjacent to the site. Building the 12,000-sq.-ft factory and 6,000-sq.-ft office block cost £14,483. The factory was designed initially for a turnover of £100,000 but the site had the potential to accommodate output of £1.5 million. The plans went through several versions for consultation with staff before they were discussed with architects. The factory was fronted by offices built in the prevailing art deco style with an impressive entrance hall and staircase. By October 1937, the site was ready for occupation.

Organising the move was a major project. The Great Western Railway (GWR) handled the contents of the London factories – 44 tons of machinery, 60 tons of stores and 14 tons of office furniture. The *Gloucestershire Echo* reported that

Great Western Railway experts have for some time been studying the layout of the Cheltenham factory, making the best means of approach, arranging for the provision of special tackle for the unloading of the machinery from the containers and providing labour for conveying the section of the machinery to the required positions in the new building.[10]

GWR estimated the task would take two weeks to complete; it took three because en route the railway shunted the trucks into a siding in Swindon and forgot about them.

The new factory would employ 100 people, 80 of whom had agreed to move from London, their relocation paid for by the company. Walter Crosweller later recalled that

those who could come doubted it was a move for the better, so we invited everyone to visit Cheltenham twice before the moving date to have a look round and see where they would like to live … We set up a housing department with the aid of one of the estate agents of this town. We found a very real shortage of artisan dwellings here. Eventually we had to appeal to the corporation for assistance, and they were good enough to let us have about a dozen

10 Gloucestershire Echo, 1 Oct 1937.

of the council houses then being built on the
Whaddon estate.[11]

The company needed more young women to
work in the office and recruited them locally well
in advance of the move. They spent six months
working for the business in London, earning a
weekly bonus on top of their usual wages, before
returning to Cheltenham. Not all of them came
back. It was Coronation year. 'They had the
pleasure of spending a nice spring and summer
in London and of being right on the spot for the
Coronation pageantry. At least two of those girls
elected to stay in London!'[12]

Cheltenham Bulletins were issued, giving
information about travel, accommodation and
housing. Initially, local people made up a quarter
of the staff employed, but, as the company
quickly expanded, that grew to more than half by
the end of 1937. Cheltenham worked its charm
on the arriving Londoners. 'The staff soon found
that living in Cheltenham was pleasant but very
different indeed from living in London … we
have found great courtesy and willing assistance
in all our dealings with the business community
of this town and with all the municipal
departments.'[13]

11 Ibid., 17 Aug 1938.
12 Ibid.
13 Ibid.

With input from employees, conditions in the
well-lit, well-ventilated and spacious purpose-built
premises were light years away from the dingy
cramped conditions of the London factories. The
company took an advanced view of smoking:
a better working environment meant less of it.
Two weeks after the move was completed, a
memorandum was sent round. 'Now that the strain
of moving is over, and better conditions prevail,
smoking must be reduced.' But the conditions
attached did not treat the sexes equally. While
senior male staff were allowed to smoke in their
offices but not continuously and not at all in
the hall or corridors, women were banned from
smoking at all during normal working hours. It was
banned too on safety grounds from the packing
department and stores.

There was space too for a sports field, where
football and cricket matches were played for many
years until production space took priority. A works
social club was set up. Workers were encouraged
to keep fit by joining the local YMCA, which gave
entry to the Montpellier Baths, where there were
gym facilities and the chance to play basketball
and badminton. To give time for people to travel
home for lunch if they wished, fifteen minutes were
added to the daily midday break. For evening
entertainment, the company offered discounted
tickets for performances by the local operatic and
dramatic society. The system of annual, seasonal
and long-service bonuses was retained.

23

2

A Springboard for Growth: 1937–61

The Cheltenham factory was a springboard for growth. As the company magazine recorded in October 1937, 'in this modern building the layout has been perfected and considerably enlarged and Mr Eaton [the works manager] can turn out more Leonards than you and we can sell at any time'. Among the innovations was a chromium plating plant that plated not only Leonard valves but also Spirax traps. It was a big step forward for the business, which would now take the opportunity given by the licensing agreement to begin winning customers overseas as well as in the UK.

The Spirax Manufacturing Company leased part of the new factory, but the days of the joint venture were ending. In 1938, to resolve continuing disagreements over royalties, James Walker and Walter Crosweller offered to buy out Clement Wells. He refused, believing the time had come for Spirax to have a life of its own without competing for attention with other agencies. Instead, Walker and Crosweller accepted Wells' offer to buy their share for the same sum, £10,800, paid in monthly instalments over the next three years. This included goodwill for the Walker Crosweller team responsible for selling Spirax traps, including Lionel Northcroft, who all moved across to the Spirax

Manufacturing Company under its new ownership in June 1939. Walker Crosweller agreed to have nothing do to with steam traps in the meantime. In fact, the company never sold another until the early 1970s when Walker Crosweller re-entered the market with stainless steel bimetallic traps under the Kero brand, but this experiment was brief, lasting at most a couple of years. Spirax moved to separate premises in St George's Road, Cheltenham, in August 1939, where the business remains today as Spirax-Sarco Engineering plc.

James Walker had two sons. The eldest, Gilbert, became a distinguished industrial economist, the first professor of economics at Birmingham University, credited with transforming the department into one of the country's main centres for modern technical economics. It was James's second son, Richard, born in 1910, who was passionate about the business. He graduated in engineering from London University before joining the company in 1932. Although father and son had an uneasy relationship, not untypical in family businesses, James Walker recognised his son's potential. Ultimately, it was Richard Walker who would drive the company's success in the years after the Second World War.

NEW

Leonard

valve –

the 21

AUTOMATIC MIXING SAVES WATER AND FUEL

The Leonard 21 is an entirely new addition to the world famous Leonard thermostatic mixing valve series. This new valve embodies the thermostat cartridge construction first introduced in the Leonard Minor. It combines elegant design with robust internal working parts. An outstanding feature is the completely restyled regulating-handle and calibrated scale-plate for quick temperature selection. Longer travel of the handle and a modified thermostat element ensure a wider temperature range and greater ease of selection. Four set screws hold the cover safely in place.

The Cheltenham
factory in 1939.

26

With the potential of the Leonard valve agreement, coupled with the impetus to sell the much greater output of the newly built factory, Richard Walker was given the task of getting exports up and running. One challenge was the factory's location; how much easier it would have been dispatching goods around the world from London's great dock system. The solution for many years was sending goods by rail for shipment from Liverpool. Later, as airline routes expanded, they would travel by road to Heathrow airport. In the brief period before the world again went to war, the company worked hard to set up a network of overseas agents, ranging from the country's nearest neighbours in Europe, such as Belgium, Romania, Denmark, Sweden and Finland, to distant colonial dominions, such as Australia, New Zealand, South Africa and Canada. Walker Crosweller had learned from the way steam traps had been sold the value of technical marketing. One recruitment advertisement asked for 'a technical journalist or advertising copywriter to help in preparation of propaganda for the export market'.[14]

In the UK, the challenge was to create a market for the Leonard valve beyond the hospital sector, where it had made its first appearance in the mid-1930s. Even before the move to Cheltenham, the company was offering to fit mixing valves on a trial basis for a wide range of different customers,

from hospitals, schools, prisons and public baths to laundries, paper works, hotels and holiday camps, in fact, anywhere hot water was in frequent use. Sales representatives were encouraged to visit the big retail stores, including Fenwick's, Marks & Spencer and Woolworth's, with their staff washing facilities and hair salons.

The time was ripe to exploit commerce and industry; the Factory Act, 1937, compelled employers to provide better washing facilities, including ample supplies of hot water. Although the Act was not implemented until 1939, many employers began making improvements and were receptive to the idea of a thermostatic mixing valve that could produce blended water at a steady temperature. Walker Crosweller was pioneering a new market with a new product and a new concept.

The quick wins were orders from commerce and industry; persistence was needed to win orders from the public sector, where budgets were more constrained and the decision-making process more bureaucratic. The list of customers lengthened – sports clubs, like Cardiff City Football Club and Lancashire County Cricket Club, and Wembley's Empire Stadium; higher education, like Nottingham University College; private estates, including Chatsworth; commercial and naval shipbuilders, from Fairfield in Glasgow to HM Chatham Dockyard. The company supplied mixing valves to public baths from Glasgow and Wolverhampton to Poplar, Finsbury and Ealing.

---

14 Ibid., 4 Apr 1940.

Leonard News, 1939.

This was one of several advertisements placed with *Punch* magazine because it was thought to include many architects amongst its readers.

Opposite The original design drawing for the Leonard steam and water mixing valve from 1939.

30

Every effort was made to promote the use of the valves for industrial processes. Mixing valves were supplied to John Smith's Tadcaster Brewery. 'We examined the [valve] for a little while,' reported J A Garrett, the salesman, 'the brewery for a longer while and sampled their products for quite a while.'[15] Other customers included Vickers-Armstrong, ICI, Kraft Cheese, HP Sauce, the Marmite Food Extract Company and Rolls-Royce.

The national rearmament programme offered opportunities, from Royal Ordnance Factories to RAF barracks, militia camps and gun ranges. The Munich crisis, as the threat of war hung in the air, provoked a rush of orders for Air Raid Precaution (ARP) stations. Valves were fitted on board Bibby Line's latest troopship and three vessels that would be lost during the next war: the battleship HMS *Hood*; the *Arandora Star*, carrying internees to Canada and torpedoed soon after leaving Liverpool; and the *Wairangi*, sunk during the battle for Malta.

Within a year of moving to Cheltenham, the UK sales force was 40-strong. Advertisements were placed not only in leading trade journals but also in the satirical magazine *Punch*, which apparently was popular with architects. All this effort paid off. The average value of monthly orders for Leonard valves rose from £210 in 1937 to more than £3,000 in 1939.

As well as making standard models, such as the Series R and Series T, already in production in the US, the company was also launching new ones. Investing in research and development paid off. As a later company magazine put it, 'There have been many strange-looking machines on our Test Bench, and our Works Manager and his staff have been walking about with that faraway look in their eyes, which comes of months of creative work … in our Research Departments both here and in the USA, we are miles ahead of any competitors and are protected at every point by patents.'[16]

Utilising the knowledge gained from steam traps, the company had its first success through the modification of an existing model to make it suitable for steam and water. The company magazine described it in March 1938 as 'a mixing valve, first, foremost and all the time. The works have concentrated their attention on designing an article that will produce blended water at a steady temperature and that will work quietly and accurately for a long time once it has been installed.' All these features – effective design, reliability and longevity – became characteristic of every version of the mixing valve produced in Cheltenham. The valves were also popular because they were easy to install, saved water and conserved heat. The Leonard steam-and-water mixing valve was a real boost in opening

15 Leonard News, July 1937.

16 Ibid., March 1940.

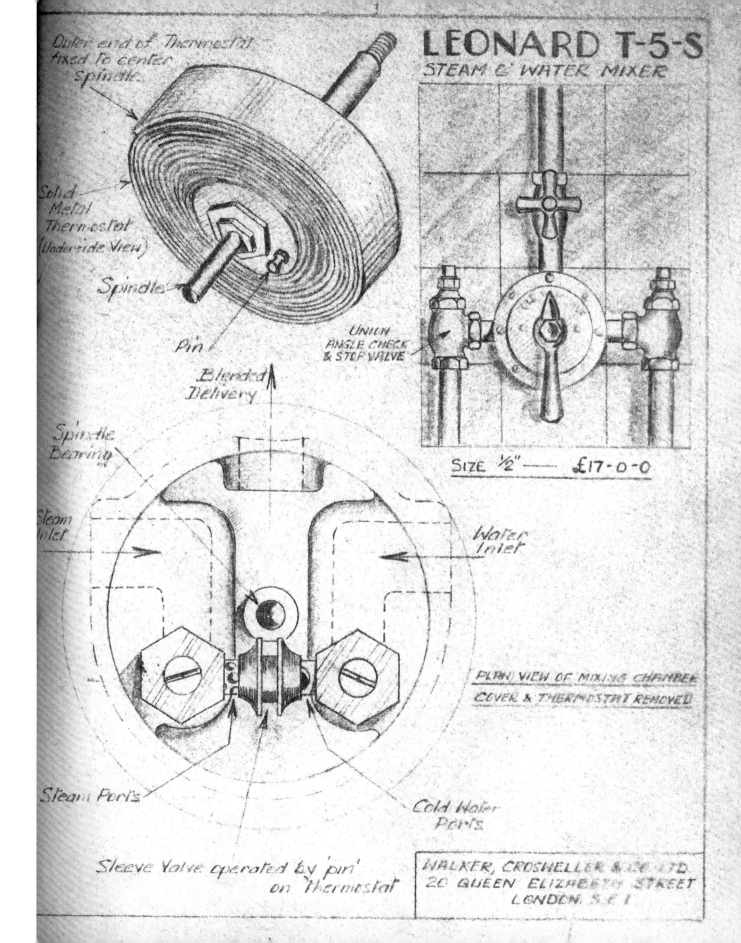

Outer end of Thermostat
fixed to center
spindle.

Solid
Metal
Thermostat
(Underside View)

Spindle

Pin

UNION
ANGLE CHECK
& STOP VALVE

LEONARD T-5-S
STEAM & WATER MIXER

SIZE ½" —— £17-0-0

Blended
Delivery

Spindle
Bearing

Steam
Inlet

Water
Inlet

PLAN VIEW OF MIXING CHAMBER
COVER & THERMOSTAT REMOVED

Steam Ports

Cold Water
Ports

Sleeve Valve operated by 'pin'
on Thermostat

WALKER, CROSHELLER & CO LTD
20 QUEEN ELIZABETH STREET
LONDON. S.E.1

Walker Crosweller Goes to War:
A Message from the Chairman, 5 Sept 1939

'Everybody knows that our work is now almost entirely Government work, but everybody may not know how near the heart of the conflict we are.

We are doing work for the War Office, the Admiralty, the Air Force, the Office of Works and other Government Departments. Leonard Valves are fitted on two of the biggest battleships in the British Navy; they form part of the equipment of all the new Ordnance Factories. We have made apparatus for the newest submarines. Militia Camps, Evacuation Camps, Defence Camps, depend on us to supply valves for their washing equipment.

I am sure it will be a source of satisfaction to everyone that our work here is so closely bound up with the country's resistance to Nazi horrors.'

up the huge industrial market, although valve orders for process applications were still limited by 1939. Within a few years, Walker Crosweller's range of Leonard thermostatic mixing valves comprised four designs in seven sizes, with an equivalent range of steam-and-water mixers. Already, the company was making a success out of specialisation, cultivating a reputation for a quality product in a niche sector, with healthy margins enabling investment in new developments and research into new applications.

By the time war was declared on 3 September 1939, the factory was producing between two and three thousand Leonard valves every month. In addition, Walker Crosweller was making a range of Arkon measuring instruments. The factory was already working overtime every night to keep up with the flood of orders for defence work. To expedite orders, those employees fortunate enough to own their own cars were asked to use them to make deliveries. Preparations were being made for around-the-clock working. By September, nine out of ten orders were for government departments as turnover, reported the company magazine, became 'astronomical'.[17] On the Sunday morning when Neville Chamberlain made his fateful announcement, workers at Walker Crosweller were busy packing and dispatching as many mixing valves as possible to gas cleansing stations and ARP posts all over the country.

The War Office placed orders for valves to be fitted to mobile showers for the troops. The company's London sales manager, Rex Boundy, witnessed a demonstration on London's Millbank where it took a squad of soldiers instructed by a

17 Ibid., Sept 1939.

Leonard News

PUBLISHED BY WALKER, CROSWELLER & CO., LTD. CHELTENHAM

1940

VOL. III. NO. 12.

DECEMBER 1939

ON A GOOD THING

ORDERS

sergeant six minutes to erect the mobile unit and another ten to get the water up to temperature. The units were used by the British Expeditionary Force in the days before Dunkirk, by the Eighth Army in North Africa and by troops fighting the Japanese in Burma. Steam-and-water mixing valves were ordered by ordnance factories for making high explosives. Thousands of mixing valves were supplied for airmen's showers and for the special salt baths used to treat badly burnt casualties. As well as mixing valves, the company supplied oil-and-water temperature regulators, which were fitted to the engines of every new motor torpedo boat. With the flood of government work, 'the emphasis, which in this establishment is always heavily on sales, shifted like lightning to production'.[18]

As government orders eased off, and then fell away sharply after early 1943, the company cultivated its industrial connections and developed new applications. Sales throughout the country were aided by growing demand from workers for better conditions as wartime pressures pushed factories to their limit. 'Better conditions,' wrote James Walker, 'mean more washing facilities, more baths, more basins, more showers.'

The sales team explored every avenue for expanding sales. In 1940 the director of a customer company whose hobby was dairy farming placed

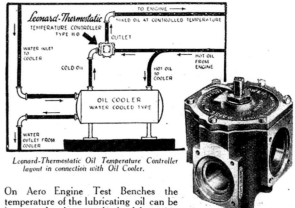

---

18 Ibid., Export Edition, Sept 1939.

Works Letter No. 99, from
Walter Crosweller, 27 July 1940

We have received complaints from eight families in Clyde Crescent of frequent singing and playing football (during second break) by the night shift … We got our Works here on the understanding that we would not become a nuisance to our neighbours.

Any unnecessary noise will, therefore, get us into trouble with the Town Authorities. Singing during night shift must, therefore, be restrained and no games or noise whatever can be allowed outside the building. It is a pity but we must keep the rules.

an order for mixing valves which would be used to wash the udders of his herd of cows. Leonard valves played a part in the pioneering development of penicillin, the first true antibiotic. In early 1944 the makers, Glaxo, used the steam-and-water mixing valves to put through the penicillin liquor, which had to be heated up rapidly.

The war accelerated the company's plans to carry out all its own machining since many of its suppliers were struggling to cope with war work. 'So, we got busy and acquired a number of capstans and other machine tools in order that we should be ready to turn to machining when our suppliers could no longer let us have finished parts.'[19] As well as the pressure to maintain supplies, the company had to manage other pressures affecting the business. Petrol rationing limited the ability of the sales team to reach customers and they were encouraged

instead to make more use of the telephone. For sales representatives operating in bomb-hit cities, particularly London, conditions were difficult, with buses diverted, underground lines closed and customer premises bombed out.

Regular bonuses were paid to compensate staff for the rising cost of living. More office staff were needed, particularly in the finance department, to administer more complex wartime contracts. The total workforce increased to 250 at its wartime peak as output rose to four times the rate in peacetime, placing machinery under great strain. The challenge was finding workers as so many men and women were on active military service or war work. Walker Crosweller lost 60 employees to military service or work in aircraft factories. Many of the new employees were local girls, who adapted quickly to learning how to operate often complicated machines. More flexible terms, including job-sharing, were offered for some posts to attract interest. The

19 Leonard News, June 1940.

The company's UK northern sales force gathered for a conference in Cheltenham on 1 May 1946 (left to right) Messrs Bartlett, Blair, Duke, Fox, Lloyd, Atkins, Radbill, Carlier, Richard, Weatherly and (kneeling) Middleton.

myriad rules and regulations introduced during wartime sometimes tripped up the company. It pleaded ignorance when it was fined in 1943 for illegally obtaining new tyres for its 21-strong fleet of motor vehicles.

Wartime pressure told on the founders. Walter Crosweller's health broke down and he retired from the business at the end of 1943. In the following year, he lost his 19-year-old son, killed in South Africa in a tragic accident while training to be an RAF pilot. For the sake of his health, he retired to the seaside town of Worthing, where he died in 1950. More trivially, James Walker was so deep in thought over business matters while he was cycling to work in March 1944 that he ignored traffic signs, for which he was later fined.

The directors believed it was important to keep up morale among the workforce. In January 1940 the staff dance at the local Palais de Danse was held, it was reported, 'in order to keep the friendly atmosphere among their staff, which was so necessary to the proper running of businesses these days'.[20] It

20 Cheltenham Chronicle, 13 Jan 1940.

doubled up as a fundraising effort to send cigarettes to the troops. This was also the year when the government asked employers to cancel all holidays stretching from Whitsun to the August bank holiday, including any leave for summer holidays, and to pay staff in lieu instead. It was unsurprising that workers should try and take respite from long hours whenever they could or that they should get into trouble for it.

A shortage of nylon stockings after clothes rationing was introduced led to a more relaxed dress code for women in the office. Asked for their views on women wearing slacks in the office, James Walker replied that the directors had no objections, 'provided that low-heeled shoes are worn with the slacks and that the high standard of decorum hitherto prevailing is maintained!'[21] Other shortages prompted further advice to staff. The typewriter was an essential part of office life, but the government banned the import of US typewriters and UK makers were unable to keep up with demand. 'All our typewriters have suddenly become precious therefore and every typist is urged to take the greatest possible care of her machine.'[22] As a result of food rationing, morning rations of milk ceased and canteen dinners became vegetarian, with priority given to production workers. The company offered allotments on the playing field to any employee

21 Memorandum, James Walker, 23 Oct 1940.
22 Memorandum, Walter Crosweller, 13 Dec 1940.

A rare image of a social outing, in this case to the seaside at Southend in 1951. Among those in the picture are Cyril Moon, Robin Olley, Tony Morgan, Percy Townley and Bill Green.

38

wishing to grow their own food and it subsidised the cost of gardening tools.

By the end of the war, the company was employing around 200 people, more than in 1939. It welcomed many demobbed servicemen back into employment and emphasised in its recruitment the factory's excellent working environment, including the canteen, central heating and a 44-hour five-day working week. Local people saw it as a good place to work. Tony Finch was dragged by his ear through the factory gates by his father to apply for a job as a packer in 1947. At the age of 17, he was earning £1 5s a week, packing products with hay into second-hand beef and pea boxes. Steadily, as conditions permitted, pre-war traditions were revived. In 1949 the New Year's Eve dinner dance organised by the entertainments committee was attended by 150 guests. There were balloons, streamers, spot dances, musical chairs and dancing to Al Kessel's Band. The sports and social club

Richard Walker Travels to Canada, from *Leonard News*, March 1949

We left London at 10 o'clock at night, we dined in Scotland at midnight, we had an early breakfast at five in the morning in Iceland, a larger and better breakfast over Denmark Strait, with the icy mountains of Greenland for scenery we had our mid-morning coffee in Labrador and our lunch with the mighty St Lawrence beneath us. At tea-time we were in Montreal but they don't have tea there. We have never seen so much ice and snow in so short a time … That was the way we went to our new office in Montreal.

arranged occasional outings, like the one to Southend in the summer of 1951, and there were children's parties in the canteen.

In a war-damaged country, counting the cost of victory, there would be a decade of austerity at home, with continued controls and rationing, as UK industry was urged to 'Export or Die!' and earn the dollars to fund imports. 'The slogan,' reported the local newspaper in June 1945, 'is taken seriously at Whaddon Works. Mixing valves were supplied to camps and a number of factories in Australia, to a large factory in India, camps in Iceland, and other products were sent in a big shipment to the Brazilian navy. The factory now has orders for a housing scheme in Cape Town and for gold mines in Johannesburg.' In 1950 there was even an order from the Shanghai Gas Works in communist China.

Pre-war agencies, like Singapore, were revived, and new ones, like Portugal and Syria, were added; the company welcomed regular visits from its overseas agents. In November 1947 Richard Walker travelled to the USA, where he persuaded the Leonard Valve Company to permit Walker Crosweller to supply valves to Canada, bringing in more valuable dollar export business. Agents were appointed in Montreal, Toronto and Halifax, and a senior sales representative, Alex Radbill, was sent

Above Loading the first part of an export order for South Africa.

Left the Cheltenham assembly shop. Taken from the company newsletter for December 1948.

out to represent the company and advise agents. In the same year, a local man was recruited as the company's technical representative in Switzerland.

By 1950, since the first Leonard valves had been made in Cheltenham, the company had halved the cost of them, whereas competing mechanical mixing valves were almost the same price. Nevertheless, there was a gap in the market for a less expensive thermostatic mixing valve. This led to the launch of the Rada valve, a smaller, neater valve, described by the company as 'a radically different design', which is perhaps where the name came from. It seems to have originated in response to competition from US valves in the Canadian market and it was to Canada that Richard Walker headed in the spring of 1950 – the headline in the local newspaper read 'Airborne in Search of Dollars' – to promote the new valve. Although it was sold both in the UK and overseas, it found its niche in the export market.

Although the company was sending valves to distant places around the world, like South Georgia and Qatar, it was in Europe as continental economies revived during the 1950s that Walker Crosweller began to find most success with exports. The strengthening West German economy was particularly fertile ground for the company. Richard Walker had pinpointed its potential in the late 1940s as the country embarked on reconstruction. An advertisement for an export assistant in that year specified applicants should

be competent in German. He visited the country in 1953, began appointing a network of agents and opened a sales office in Frankfurt in 1955, which became a subsidiary company in 1958. The company launched an advertising campaign before setting up a sales organisation, capitalising on the many enquiries that resulted. 'The Germans are universally regarded as model export salesmen who can deliver the goods,' said Richard Walker a few years later. 'I set out deliberately to challenge their home market … Competition shouldn't worry anybody. It was in Germany that our company met its fiercest competition and Germany is now our most successful market.'[23]

While export sales were valuable – and appreciated by the government – the company relied on UK sales, where it remained the leader in a market it had largely created. The decade after the end of the war was challenging as the scarcely solvent country slowly rebuilt. This was summed up in the company magazine during the atrocious winter of 1947. 'Coal shortage, electricity cuts, the economic situation and so on – one would almost think the morning's news was provided to distract our attention from the size of the bacon ration.'[24] The company was preparing, it said, for the revival of 'the great pre-war markets for water mixers – schools, hospitals,

23 Financial Times, 21 August 1961.
24 Leonard News, January 1947.

public baths'[25], but this was slow in coming. It was also looking to the continuing trend, begun pre-war and accelerated by the war, towards better working conditions. It had ambitions to persuade equipment manufacturers to incorporate mixing valves in post-war designs. A major advertising campaign, 'Getting Hot Water', was launched. In a seller's market, the company took the opportunity to press customers to eliminate many of the problems that had always dogged installation, from rotten pipework to inadequate water supplies. Rising demand allowed the company to take advantage of growing economies of scale and make a better valve for less money.

Since several key markets identified by the company, including schools and hospitals, relied on public spending, they were prone to sudden

cutbacks whenever economic circumstances deteriorated. When the National Health Service was founded in 1948, it was seen as a great opportunity, and sales representatives were dispatched to contact the principal architects involved in planning new hospitals. But investment in the new service was uneven and progress was slow. The school building programme finally got off the ground during 1949, rewarding the persistence of all those sales representatives for the time they had spent cultivating local authority architects. It helped that the Ministry of Education insisted on thermostatic mixing valves for basins and showers. But, within a year, orders slumped because of government cutbacks. Conversely, the eruption of the crisis in Korea in 1950 prompted a flurry of defence-related orders, once again including mixing valves for mobile shower units.

41

25 Ibid.

The NHS became an important customer of the company.

The company recognised the danger of over-reliance on government orders and worked hard to spread business across several different sectors. Resellers, including plumbers' and builders' merchants, were becoming more important, contributing a third of monthly sales. They grumbled about the miserly discount they received but were eager to stock the leading mixing valve on the market. In the early 1950s, other customers included salmon smokers, chemical plants, power stations, oil refineries, breweries, car makers, bakeries, bedding makers, farms and original equipment manufacturers. As economic conditions improved, and the market shifted in favour of buyers, the company noted how customer expectations were changing. 'He is already getting hard to please; delivery from stock is scarcely quick enough; the price must be closely compared with other offers; any hitch in our negotiations puts him off.'[26]

It was the prospect of the abolition of the last wartime controls that whetted the appetite of the Walker Crosweller salesmen. The rationing of sweets finally ended in February 1953. 'With everybody in Whaddon Works eating Mars bars and the like, we shall be doing our bit to keep up demand.'[27] Within a couple of years, with rising public spending, orders from central and

26 Ibid., January 1953.
27 Ibid., February 1953.

Launching a New Product: The Rada Brand, *Leonard News*, September 1950

When a new design finally leaves the Drawing Office and passes onto the Production Shop, the DO boys can get on with practising their skittles, but in the Shop they start scratching their heads about how they are going to make the new product. It cannot just be thrown on to the machines using the old tools. New tools are wanted and new ways of handling them have to be thought out.

When the Production Shop has finished, the new valve is handed over to the Sales Department and to them in turn it brings a new set of problems demanding new methods for their solution. Sales policy and sales techniques must be examined and overhauled to see that they fit the new valve.

local government began to multiply, not only for schools and hospitals, but for fire stations, public baths and sports field changing rooms. Strengthening sales led to the expansion of the London sales team to cover the Home Counties and beyond and for the first time a sales manager was appointed for Scotland. The company's approach to advertising was refreshed under a new publicity manager, and investment in new equipment transformed its direct mail campaigns.

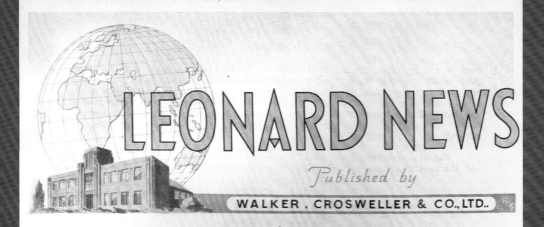

LEONARD NEWS

Published by

WALKER, CROSWELLER & CO., LTD..

VOLUME 11.   NUMBER 9.   SEPTEMBER, 1950.

RADA TO THE ARCHITECTS.

When a new design finally leaves the Drawing Office and passes on to the Production Shop, the D.O. boys can get on with practising their skittles, but in the Shop they start scratching their heads about how they are going to make the new product.   It cannot just be thrown on to the machines using the old tools.   New tools are wanted and new ways of handling them have to be thought out.

When the Production Shop has finished, the new valve is handed over to the Sales Department and to them in turn it brings a new set of problems demanding new methods for their solution.   Sales policy and sales technique must be examined and overhauled to see that they fit the new valve.

The first job we have to do with the Rada, therefore, is to examine its qualities and work out the sales methods by which we can make full use of these to develop and expand our market.

In looking at the Rada we see one of its most valuable assets - its appearance.   Smaller and neater, it is a good companion for the most expensive bathroom fittings and far better looking than any other thermostatic mixing valve, whether Leonard or other make.   Architects are interested in the look of the fittings they specify and therefore the Rada should be on its way to every architect's desk in your territory.   Having something new to talk about enables us to present ourselves afresh, so to speak, to architects, to reawaken their interest in thermostatic mixing valves and keep them thinking about them for school, hospital or industrial jobs.

Our advertising drives hard on this road and full page advertisements in the Builder, Architects Journal and Plumbing Journal, and the new pamphlet mailed to every architect, will be of immense assistance to us.   But we must follow up, above all promptly, the interest created by our advertisements and seize every opportunity of getting effective interviews to demonstrate the new valve.

The introduction of the Rada to architects and specifying authorities

The Leonard 72 valve was launched in 1959 and later rebadged under the Mira brand.

44

A Sales Visit to a US Army Air Force Station in Norfolk, *Leonard News*, March 1951

This visit had all the charm and excitement of an attempt to penetrate behind the Iron Curtain, the chief difference being that I did return. Security police, apparently modelling themselves on Russian counterparts, are a little wearing – one needs considerable restraint and a sense of humour which should be carefully kept in check until the last barriers are behind one – these people take themselves very seriously. Brandishing various passes, I eventually got to the Holy of Holies.

When, in 1955, the company magazine listed a handful of famous customers, from Buckingham Palace to the Bank of England, it set out why the company was successful. 'We can count these famous people among our customers because for years we have resisted all temptations to deviate from our chosen policy of specialising in thermostatic mixing valves. Specialists not only in their design and manufacture but also in their uses and applications … we are able to give the customer sound advice on the use of our product before he buys it … we take the trouble to see that he gets the right mixing valve for his job

… we look after him after he has installed the Leonard … these are the reasons, together with good design and workmanship, which spread the reputation of our product so far and wide.'[28]

The factory expanded to meet rising demand. By 1950, production was spilling out into second-hand army huts pending permission to construct the first extension since the factory opened in 1937. Five years later, as record sales and output were achieved, foundations were laid for a new building as large as the original factory. By the

28 Ibid., September 1944.

An aerial view of the Cheltenham factory in 1958.

end of the decade, more than 300 people were working for Walker Crosweller. The works and the drawing office continued to make improvements to existing models and come up with new ones, more efficient and less expensive, such as the Leonard 3, launched in 1952. In 1955 the company patented the Unatap, designed in collaboration with the Building Research Station; a single tap mixing hot and cold water through a spray at a temperature selected by turning the knob, it cut the cost of hot water and saved large quantities of water. Just as innovative was the Leonard 72, introduced in 1959, the first thermostatic shower valve capable of providing satisfactory showering under UK supply pressures. In the same year came the Leonard 621 and 21 mixing valves equipped with cartridges to control the flow of water.

By the second half of the 1950s, a time when, according to Prime Minister Harold Macmillan, 'most of our people have never had it so good', almost every education authority in the UK specified Leonard mixing valves, they were standard on naval and passenger ships, and used by several government departments. By comparison with the first half of the decade, Walker Crosweller's average annual profits had doubled.

3

A Revolutionary Period: 1961–75

This was a revolutionary period for Walker Crosweller. The company advanced on many fronts but the most important was its deliberate move into domestic showers. Just as it had established the UK market for thermostatic mixing valves, so Walker Crosweller effectively created the UK domestic shower market. The Mira brand launched in 1962 and became the UK's leading shower brand. The decision transformed the business and laid the foundations for the company that exists today.

Before that momentous event, Walker Crosweller became a public company. On 24 August 1961, the company offered the public 30 per cent of its one million five-shilling ordinary shares for 8s 6d each. Investors were enthusiastic about the flotation, backing an established engineering company with a good trading record, which had seen sales rise by 20 per cent during the previous year. The issue was oversubscribed nine times.

Becoming a public company opened the door of the boardroom to non-family members for the first time. While James Walker and his son Richard remained chairman and managing director respectively, C F Taylor and Derrick Launchbury joined the board. Taylor had joined the business in 1942 after being invalided out of active service,

working his way through sales to become sales director. He had worked hard to develop Walker Crosweller's exports to Europe and Scandinavia. Launchbury joined the company as a junior clerk in 1939, interrupting his career for war service between 1942 and 1946. He progressed through the accounts department and became company secretary in 1957. The directors were supported by a senior management team, which included M E Brooks as general manager of the home sales division, R Harrison as works manager and T Evans as production manager.

When James Walker died in 1963, Richard added the role of chairman. One of his father's legacies, other than the firm foundations of the business, was the Macfarlane Walker Trust. Its aims were to relieve poverty and hardship among employees and retirees of Walker Crosweller & Co. Ltd, provide recreational and social welfare facilities in Gloucestershire, support educational facilities for scientific research, and encourage music, drama and fine arts. It remains in existence today.

There were several reasons why the business needed to raise more capital. Growth demanded more working capital, particularly to support Walker Crosweller's flourishing export trade, which

Unatap

SfB 53

UDC 696·4

UW20/3   OCTOBER 1968

Save water heating costs: add greater hygiene

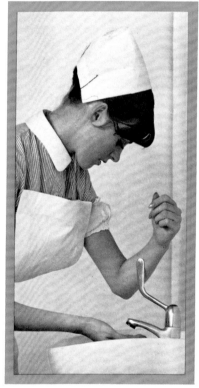

Economy of Water
Independent tests have proved up to 86% savings of HOT water! A Unatap can be set to give 4 to 5 pints per minute only, just enough for hand washing.

Economy of Time
Tests have shown that hand washing with a Unatap takes only 30% of the time taken with conventional taps. Remember: one quick turn of the single knob gives both temperature and flow.

Economy of Hot-Water Storage
Because of a much reduced usage, the size of hot water storage can be smaller.

Economy of Pipework and Fittings
A small water usage leads to smaller diameter pipework, and smaller and less costly wastepipes and traps.

Economy of Space
Smaller and therefore less costly wash-basins can be used. Therefore, more people can wash in the same space or the same number of people in less space.

Economy of Planning
Low flows of water mean less pipe-sizing problems for the consulting engineer. In today's taller and taller buildings the problem of increasing water-storage weight or higher and higher capacity pumps becomes a severe problem. The Unatap needs less water so less water is stored (or pumped), with correspondingly less weight and storage space (or pump size) problems.
And in addition to all these economies, the Unatap is:

More Hygienic
Hand-washing under running water is the doctor's way, the better way. It means, too, cleaner basins, easier hand-washing.
Both Unatap types 11 & 24 are UK Ministry of Health selected designs.

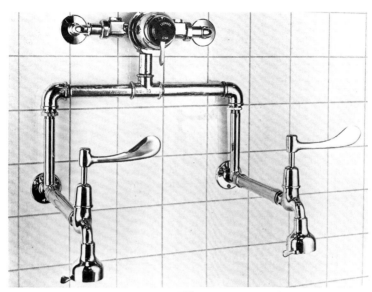

surgeon's elbow fitting

for use with leonard thermostatic mixing valves

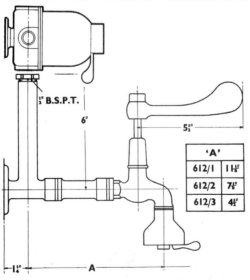

$\frac{1}{2}''$ B.S.P.T.

6"

5$\frac{1}{2}''$

'A'	
612/1	1 1$\frac{1}{8}''$
612/2	7$\frac{1}{2}''$
612/3	4$\frac{1}{2}''$

1$\frac{1}{4}''$

A

Comprising $\frac{1}{2}''$ elbow-action bibcock with spray jet attachment, L shaped connecting pipe with wall bracket and variable extension 'A'. All in polished chrome.

Walker Crosweller and Company Limited, Cheltenham

LW304/2 P.64

Throughout this period the NHS remained
an important customer for the company.

now accounted for 40 per cent of sales. Richard Walker pointed out that overseas credit could be extended for as long as 120 days. More capacity was needed in the factory. Another bay had been added recently, taking floorspace to 34,000 square feet, and there were plans for a new combined factory and office block.

Work on the new extension began not a moment too soon. With booming sales, more space was needed to overcome lengthening delivery times and a mounting backlog of orders. Finished at the end of 1964, it also helped the company to meet its objective of bringing in-house as much of the production process as possible. The extension housed a pressure diecasting plant to ensure a steady supply of brass castings for the Leonard, Arkon and Mira ranges, which allowed the company to make more accurate casting, save on finishing work and reduce costs. (In 1965 the company also set up its own plastic injection moulding plant.)

Richard Walker and his team were already thinking about investing in the domestic shower market, which was essentially non-existent at the time. The time was opportune. The country was more prosperous and people had more money to spend. Bathrooms were seen as an indispensable part of every home, even though they were still absent in many older houses. Walker Crosweller had been harbouring the ambition to sell domestic showers since before the war but never considered

The Leonard 72 mixing valve was the company's best selling product throughout the 1960s.

SfB 53
UDC 696·4
MAY 1968

Leonard 72 thermostatic shower combinations & fittings

Showers – in the home, factory, school, hotel, hospital and aboard ship – are increasingly regarded as a civilised necessity and pleasure. Ideally, each shower should have its own thermostatic mixing valve: and we illustrate here combinations centred on the Leonard 72, plus illustrations of separate fittings that may be used in grouped showers.

it a viable proposition. Historically, British households suffered from low water pressure, a major disadvantage for gravity-fed showers since most homes simply did not have the headroom above their bathrooms to create the necessary flow.

This changed after the war. By the 1960s, improvements made it possible to introduce domestic showers with as little as three feet head of water pressure. Walker Crosweller was the first company to capitalise on this opportunity.

A company show stand at Olympia in the 1960s.

Richard Walker's vision was to offer resellers and installers a complete package containing all the necessary parts, from control valves to shower fittings, for installing a domestic shower. At the 1961 Olympia Building Exhibition, the company launched two valves, a thermostatic mixing valve and a mechanical valve, designed to operate at low pressure, together with its first shower fitting.

The Leonard 72 half-inch thermostatic mixing valve, it was reported in 1964, 'is a fashion maker: it is introducing people to the thermostatic control of water suppliers for the first time, and in the case of potentially large users, it is not only selling itself, but it is opening the door for other members of the Leonard family.'[29] It was the first thermostatic valve to combine temperature and flow control 'in one compact, elegant and recessible unit'.[30] The valve was a great success, accounting for 64 per cent of all mixing valves sold by the company in 1963, although most orders came not from resellers or installers – the direct-to-consumer market did not yet exist – but from institutions such as schools and hospitals. It was also installed in the leading Cunard liner, the *Queen Elizabeth*.

The mechanical valve originated from an existing product, called the Mixwell, licensed

29 Ibid., May 1964.
30 Ibid., June 1962.

from the Danish valve manufacturer Broen. It was not long before the company developed its own version, launched under a new name as the Mira mixing valve, later better known as the Mira 8. Both products featured on the company's stand at the 1961 Building Exhibition. By the following year, the company could claim that 'our newest arrival, the Mira, is becoming more and more firmly established'.[31] It was described in one trade journal as 'a major technical breakthrough for the designers and should give a big boost to the growing demand for domestic showers'.[32] It was more popular than the Leonard 72 because it was simpler and cheaper. The lack of thermostatic control was not a major concern for those few consumers who wanted a shower; the sudden rise in temperature if another cold tap was turned on in the house was largely tolerated.

Shower fittings were added to complete the range of products for the domestic market. Some years previously, the company had declared: 'We have always kept clear of handling shower fittings, because they are a cut-price line, and we have never found one on the market which had especial features.' In 1961, however, the company made its first shower fitting, with a swivel joint and easy-to-clean rose, and a reversible shower arm, simple to pack and easy to assemble. But this venture proved

31 Ibid.
32 Plumbing & Journal of Heating, February 1963.

The Mira brand was launched in 1961. The Mira 8 was the first shower advertised on UK television.

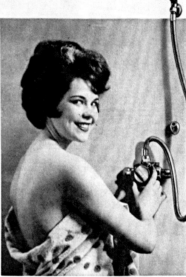

to complete YOUR bathroom

the luxury of dual shower control

This new shower tap has two dials. Set the water force with the black outer dial. Set the temperature by the grey centre control. Then enjoy a perfect shower. Elegant and compact, the Mira needs no elaborate plumbing or special water supplies. It is simple to operate and easy to install. The Mira brings to YOUR bathroom the trouble-free shower you've always wanted.

The advantages of Mira are available for your handbasin, too—no more fiddling with two taps.

inner for temperature

outer for force

mira
SHOWER TAP

Ask to see the Mira at any good builders' merchants.

WALKER CROSWELLER OF CHELTENHAM

short-lived since the company was factoring shower fittings from an external supplier by 1968.

Design was a paramount consideration for the Walker Crosweller team. For Richard Walker, design was one of the key functions of any manufacturer. He was proud that the company was inventive and resourceful in design. A L Hancock, the company's technical director, stressed simplicity in design and insisted that improving a product should never make it more complex. Every new design was submitted to the Council for Industrial Design, which in 1964 selected the Leonard 72 for an exhibition held in Moscow as a showcase for British design.

To promote this initiative, the company had 'intensified its campaign for bathing by showers and there is no doubt about it that showers have come to stay'.[33] In 1963 the company launched 'the first large-scale campaign for showers for the home', featuring the Mira mixing tap. 'The firm,' said one trade journal 'is making a strong bid to influence the general public towards the pleasures, convenience, economy and space saving of showers in the home.' Marketing the Mira 8 directly to consumers was a bold move when traditionally they had relied on the recommendation of a plumber. Part of the campaign was an innovative publication, *The Daily Shower*, aimed at the DIY enthusiast, which was soon joined by *The Mira*

Mirror. In 1966 came the Shower Information Bureau, which issued an illustrated booklet on showers, *A Shower in Your Home*. There were sales offices and showrooms in London, Manchester and Glasgow, where customers could see the products on display. As the market grew, the company's advertising became more ambitious, and in 1968 the first shower advertised on British television was the Mira 8.

The company never forgot the plumber and installer. In line with Richard Walker's vision, Walker Crosweller wanted to make it easy for plumbers to opt for its own brands, offering as complete packages, mounted on card, heat-sealed in polythene and packed in cartons, differing combinations of control valve, risers and shower roses. In 1964 the company's campaign to promote showers, this time based around the Leonard 72, was backed by the Registered Plumbers' Association. By the end of the year, one or other of the shower combination packages made up 60 per cent of all orders for the Leonard 72.

The merchants were also important. As early as December 1958, the company was stressing that 'merchandising is a very specialised form of selling'.

Selling to a sanitary wholesaler or taking a stock order is only a small part of the battle. The good salesman then sets about ensuring that stock turns over quickly. He helps to get good showroom and window displays. He

33 Leonard News, December 1963.

The Mira Name

There are two stories about the origins of the name Mira. The first suggests it came from a shortening of the name of Richard Walker's daughter, Mirabel. The second comes from Alan Schuman, who joined Walker Crosweller in 1950 as a technical sales representative and was involved with Mira sales from the beginning. The name, he said, was taken by James Walker from the Latin *mirabilis*, meaning amazing, wonderful or marvellous, with which his son Richard was so taken that he called his daughter Mirabel, or 'wonderful daughter'.

trains the merchant's showroom and outside sales staff to appreciate and recommend his product. He gets the counter staff on his side too so that they can talk knowledgeably to the plumbers and installers. Finally, he does all he can to get customers into the merchant's premises by means of helping to organise special promotions.[34]

By 1971 the company was holding Shower Expert Training seminars for staff from builders' merchants under sales training supervisor George Sandham.

A separate sales organisation was set up to promote domestic showers – H Billingham became the first sales representative in 1962 – and the company believed that its premium product was the Leonard 72. 'The use of the shower in all situations,' claimed the company magazine, 'is really on the increase … Showers save money on initial equipment, on installation costs and on running costs. And, of course, the best shower of all is the Leonard thermostatic shower.'[35] Yet although the Leonard 72 was an undoubted success, its niche lay with institutions. 'The real heart, soul and body of the Leonard Thermostatic Valve market is the "one-offs" for the bakery round the corner, the school the other end of town, and so on … developing a real wide circle of satisfied customers each bringing along their repeat orders.'[36]

It was the Mira mechanical mixing valve, requiring variations in temperature to be corrected manually, that took hold in the domestic market. The Mira brand was the first independent product range developed by Walker Crosweller since its licensing agreement with the Leonard Valve Company. To consolidate its success, it was developed and marketed through a new company, Miraflo Ltd, formed in 1963. By 1974, when Miraflo was absorbed within the parent company, the brand was firmly established.

53

34 Ibid., December 1958.

35 Ibid., December 1964.
36 Ibid., June 1962.

Richard Walker

Richard Walker was the energy behind Walker Crosweller for several decades. Joining the company in the shadow of his autocratic father, he masterminded the export business before and after the war prior to taking over as managing director. He drove the company's creation of the domestic shower market in the UK, which gave it a leading position it has never lost. He could seem remote and intimidating to some employees, mainly because they rarely had any direct contact with him. When Roy Minett was first summoned to his office, he found the managing director's desk placed on a dais, giving him the advantage of looking down on you. But, said Roy, Richard Walker 'was a wonderful man, a gentle sort of man, very softly spoken'. When he was on site, he would walk through the factory every day, and he knew everybody's name and the names of their children. As an indication of how seriously the company took the employment of local people, Richard Walker regarded it as a personal insult if those children didn't join the company when they grew up.' He was an unceasingly enthusiastic exponent of engineering and the need to train young engineers, which led the company to develop its outstanding apprenticeship programme. Active in the wider industry as president of the British Valve Manufacturers' Association in 1966–67 and of the Comité Européen de l'Industrie de la Robinetterie in 1971–72, he was awarded the OBE in 1973. He retired from the business as chairman in 1979 and died in 2000. Derrick Launchbury, for many years company secretary, knew Richard Walker well. 'Richard was quite gentle but you didn't argue with him, because he was the boss. He took the company where it needed to go and had the courage to open up the domestic shower market. He was a pioneer.'

Richard Walker
(1910–2000).

Richard Walker with Her Royal Highness Princess Anne.

With two outstanding new products, the factory became busier than ever. In February 1964, reported the company, 'business is booming and we are riding on the crest of a buoyant wave'.[37] There was enormous potential in the UK's domestic shower market; in 1965 only 3 per cent of UK homes had showers. At the same time, the company was striving to develop new models as well as improve existing models, although these were sometimes delayed because of pressure on the factory to meet rising demand. This was the case with the launch in 1965 of the Mira 10, a non-thermostatic bath filler/shower mixing valve, replacing both taps; and the revised version of the Leonard 72

thermostatic shower valve with independent flow and temperature control.

Another major product was the Unatap, introduced in 1962. 'The new Unatap is one of the best products we have produced.'[38] A single tap mixing hot and cold water through a spray at a temperature selected by turning a knob, it saved water and energy by economising on the use of hot water. It was another example of fine industrial design, as one trade review noted: 'The "technology" of ordinary things such as water taps is often underrated. The Unatap, designed and made by Walker Crosweller of Cheltenham, is actuated by light pressure of wrist or elbow to select the desired temperature of a spray

37 Ibid., February 1964.

38 Ibid., June 1962.

the unatap saves water and water heating costs

The Unatap is a single tap which mixes hot and cold water and delivers a spray at the temperature you select by turning the knob. It solves two major problems one or both of which affect all parts of the world. Firstly, it cuts the fuel costs of hot water ; secondly, it saves large quantities of water.

The Unatap originated in tests carried out with the U.K. Building Research Station. In one later installation test supervised independently, it was reported that the saving of total water was 78 per cent. Even more impressive the saving of hot water—86 per cent. This major economy is reflected equally in the cost of heating the water.

From these figures you can calculate how long it will take for the savings to pay for the cost of the installation.

EASY TO USE

Turning the Unatap knob opens or closes the flow and selects the temperature. The spray force is constant, but the temperature can be turned to the hottest water available. The more hygienic and refreshing nature of spray washing is obvious and enjoyable to the user.

of water at a constant rate.'[39] It proved ideal in hospitals and other settings where hygiene was a priority. More than a thousand were supplied to the Coventry and Warwick Hospital in 1966, for example, and over 1,600 to the redeveloped St Thomas' Hospital in London in 1971. It was also specified for army barracks, schools and hotels.

The company met demand by investing in new plant and equipment, research and development, training and improved production methods. Impressed by the productivity of factories he had visited in the USA, Richard Walker adopted work study to drive greater efficiency in the Cheltenham factory. The advantages, he said, were 'simplification of the method of work and the introduction of new and better equipment'.[40] In 1963, which was promoted as Productivity Year by the government, the company, already noted for its good labour relations and productivity, featured in 'The Box on the Wall', one of a series of films, *Look at Life*, made by the Rank Organisation. It showed how applying work study to the Leonard thermostatic valve assembly saved time and effort. Richard Walker arranged screenings of the film for all his employees at the local Odeon. Stars included Fred Kerr, chief work study engineer, Derek Moth and Pamela Brown. In the same year, the company was one of the top eleven firms

39 The Mercantile Guardian, September 1966.
40 Business Journal for Management, March 1963.

Thermostatic mixing valves and spray mixing taps undergoing final inspection and cleaning in the factory in 1961.

receiving awards from the British Safety Council for their exemplary record. This was partly due to a work study project that had produced a safer floor plan in collaboration with shopfloor workers.

Richard Walker and his technical director Ron Harrison were advocates of expedient automation. Flow production, adopted for making and assembling thermostatic valves, kept down costs and freed employees for other work. Capstan lathes and the polishing process were automated, and the company ingeniously adapted a fruit and

Apprentice Memories:
Roger Tallis

In 1963 Roger Tallis began his apprenticeship as part of his Higher National Diploma (HND) college course, dividing his time between college tuition and instruction in the company's training school under training manager Alf Hurworth. In the machine shop, he helped to wind thermostatic bimetallic coils and spent time setting up machines. While most machines were still manual, some lathes had been converted to automatic operation. There were also a handful of very noisy automatic machines supplied by the German maker Index. The valve assembly area comprised half a dozen benches under foreman Roy Davis and chargehand Frank Coates, who had three brothers working in the company, Jim (Arkon drawing office), Albert and John (toolmakers). Everyone had to clock in and, Roger recalled, anyone a minute late or more was docked half an hour's pay. At ten o'clock every morning, the factory buzzer went and everyone from the factory took their tea break in the canteen run by the fearsome Betty Grubb. She challenged anyone she spotted leaving food on their plate, which she regarded as an insult to her cooking. Latecomers had their meals kept in the oven, which were often so hot that the gravy formed a tidemark around the plates.

Like many Walker Crosweller apprentices, Roger remained with the company for the rest of his career, eventually retiring as new product development director in 2006.

Press cutting from the *Gloucestershire Echo*, 1989.

Richard Walker with a group of prizewinning apprentices in 1962.

vegetable packing machine for packing valves and shower fittings more cheaply and quickly.

The company also invested in emerging technology; the first computer, installed at the end of 1966, improved production efficiency and stock control, reducing stock levels and improving delivery times. In 1971, Walker Crosweller became the first UK company to install an acoustic chamber to meet standards for noise generated by mixing valves required by the West German market.

For Richard Walker, training was an integral part of greater efficiency. Technical courses were organised to keep employees up to date with new production techniques and processes. More rapid output led to the transfer of some functions from

the shopfloor to newly created posts, like quality control engineers. To organise an extended training programme, for all employees from apprentices to senior managers, the first training instructor was appointed in 1965.

Although the company had run apprenticeships for many years, it was during the 1960s, in response to a shortage of local skilled labour, that the foundations were laid for the apprenticeship programme which still flourishes today. The number of apprentices recruited annually increased from three in 1964 to ten in 1966. By then, the training team comprised a training manager, works training officer and one full-time and five part-time instructors. An existing building was converted into

Walker Crosweller Apprentices Association

We will now devote in each edition a double page for THE WALKER CROSWELLER APPRENTICES ASSOCIATION

This Association was formed in 1966 and has been gaining in strength every year. The Annual General Meeting was held recently and in our next issue we will picture the new officers for the Association.

By far the biggest outside project this year has been the transformation of a company van to a gleaming mini-bus, through the able direction of Apprentice Supervisor, David Gregory and Apprentice Instructor, Colin Watkins. Our pictures show the changeover from start to finish, together with the canoe trailer. The Association sent a team during the Spring Bank Holiday to the the 100 mile River Trent canoe test,

an endurance course from Penkridge near Wolverhampton to Newark, Nottinghamshire. This course was a real challenge; all our teams

finished except one who retired suffering from exposure.

a
In the mini-bus from left to right,
Apprentices:
David Wilcox
Andrew Page
Edward Willington
David Anger
Gary Swadling
Stuart Gourlay
Kevin James
Adrian Lockstone

b
Roger Hands - leading hand from the Tool Room putting the finishing touches to the Mini-bus.

c
Andrew Berry and Robert Green fix the panels and paint respectively,

e
Peter McGeachan steadies his craft.

f

d
(Left to right)
Nicholas Holtom,
Stuart Gourlay
Peter McGeachan
Adrian Lockston
and kneeling in front
Tony Almond.

g
Assembling for the start.

Unloading the canoes from the transport.

h
GO! (100 miles to the finishing line, phew!)

The Apprentices Association was founded in 1966 and for many years one annual event was the 100 mile canoe test. These pictures show one of these events on the Trent.

an apprentice training centre, where apprentices spent the first year of a five-year apprenticeship learning the basics about engineering, followed by two years on the shopfloor. They also spent some time training with other engineering companies. The last two years were concentrated on preparing apprentices for the line of work they had expressed as a preference when they finished their training. In 1973, for example, the nine apprentices who completed their training filled roles as setters, draughtsmen, production development engineers, toolmakers, work study engineers, tooling engineers and skills inspectors. The training team of that time, recalled one apprentice, Nick Reichelt, were always helpful and supportive, from Gordon Cavanagh, the personnel officer, to Derrick Peacey, the innovative training manager, and George Collins, the apprentice training officer.

The company encouraged as many people as possible to fulfil their potential. Pete Green took up his apprenticeship in 1969 because he liked the emphasis given to personal development. The training manager at the time, Mike Branch, believed in delivering a broad-based training. Part of Pete's apprenticeship, for instance, included two weeks at the activity centre on Drake's Island, Plymouth; a course at the National Outdoor Centre at Plas y Brenin in North Wales and taking part in the Duke of Edinburgh's award scheme. All these were part of the most recent developments in outdoor education in the UK and it was

far-sighted of Walker Crosweller to encourage apprentices to participate.

Most of these outdoor activities were arranged through the Apprentice Association, formed in 1966 as more apprentices were recruited. Run by the apprentices themselves, it helped to forge friendships and create bonds, which it was hoped would influence them to stay with the company for the long term. Many did spend their careers with the business, often retiring as senior managers or directors. Richard Walker was keen to give managerial responsibilities to able and qualified young men in their 20s, which he contrasted with his own experience before the war when no one was given a chance until they were at least in their early 30s.

Apprentices also had the opportunity to study for further qualifications. In 1969, for instance, Nicholas Beck became the first Walker Crosweller apprentice to graduate in mechanical engineering, an external London university degree achieved through a sandwich course with North Gloucestershire Technical College.

An apprentice marked the completion of his training by receiving his indentures at the annual prize-giving, presided over by Richard Walker. It was held for several years in local hotels, until a new canteen was built, which was big enough to hold the entire workforce if necessary. It was an evening event, attended by parents and senior management as well as prize-winners, with refreshments to follow.

Apprentice Memories:
Nick Reichelt and Martin Bull

Nick Reichelt was 'a fresh-faced 16-year-old school leaver' when he joined Walker Crosweller in August 1970 as a technical apprentice on a five-year course. He had identified three local firms, but it was the manufacturing processes – 'I could see a product made from start to finish' – that attracted him to the business. In his year, there were seven Walker Crosweller apprentices and one from another local firm. Martin Bull joined Walker Crosweller as an apprentice as a 16-year-old school leaver in 1973. His father had suggested he should apply to Walker Crosweller as well as other leading local engineering firms. He accepted the offer from Walker Crosweller because it was a smaller, more intimate business than Dowty, the much larger engineering

business in the town. 'It was the right choice. It was very much a family-oriented company.' There were nine apprentices in Martin's year.

Their first year was spent in the small wooden building that was the company's training school. 'We were kept slightly isolated from the rest of the factory,' Nick recalled. At lunchtime, everyone played football on the playing field. On Friday afternoons, the first-year apprentices finished early so they could take part in sport, often playing five-a-side football at the local boys' club.

Through block release at the local college, Martin was able to study for his Ordinary National Certificate (ONC) and later his Higher National Certificate (HNC). His next two years were spent gaining experience in various

The company has fostered a strong apprenticeship programme for many years. The group photograph of the 1975 prizewinning apprentices shows (standing from left to right) Graham Tavener, Joseph McDonnell, Raymond Gould, Raymond Wegryn, Howard Newman, Anthony Richardson, Jeffrey Tibbles and Nicholas Reichelt, with (seated) Richard Walker and guest speaker local businessman John Threadingham.

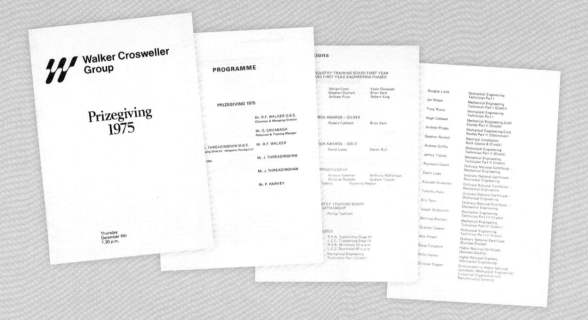

departments around the company. There were opportunities for production training, including the foundry where brass and stainless diecasting took place; plastic injection moulding; a polishing and plating shop; a tool room; an experimental workshop; and a huge machine shop, filled with a hundred machines – manual, semi-automatic and automatic – including a few CNC machines, which was advanced for the time. The Arkon division, making measuring instruments, and the plastic injection moulding department had just been relocated to units on the Kingsditch Lane industrial estate.

Through the Apprentice Association, both Nick and Martin went on a residential activity course at Plas Y Brenin in North Wales, canoeing, climbing and walking – and, recalled Martin, meeting girls. He went twice on the annual 100-mile canoeing test, organised by the National Boys' Clubs of Great Britain, once along the Wye, once along the Trent. They both took part in the Duke of Edinburgh's award scheme, Nick gaining the silver award, Martin the gold.

For Martin Bull, it was through the apprenticeship programme that the company built up its skilled workforce. Apprentices, he said, were 'one of the mainstays for craft workers and technical skills'. Like Nick and Martin, many stayed on with the company – 'there was a peppering of apprentices throughout the company from shopfloor to senior management'. After their training, Martin moved into materials control before spending the last part of his career in health and safety; while Nick became an assembly chargehand, the start of a career in production management, which culminated in his role as manufacturing engineering manager prior to his retirement in 2016.

The Apprentice Training Centre at Mira, 1967.
Among those pictured are, from left to right,
John Woodward (left middle), John Stevens,
George Collins (training instructor, in white
coat), Dave Gregory (right back), Peter Zachach,
Derek Sohey and Roger Hands (left back),
Mike Heale (back, next to Roger Hands).

The 1964 factory extension taking shape.

After the Second World War, when women had worked in the factory, they were confined almost entirely to jobs in administration until the 1970s. Many of them worked in the typing pool, indispensable in an era before word processing and personal computers. They had their own commercial training programme and they were encouraged to study for qualifications in commercial subjects as well as typing and shorthand.

Relations between employees and management were so good that they were singled out as exceptional by one Swiss newspaper in 1961. The *Neue Zürcher Zeitung* noted that unlike many British workers, those employed by Walker Crosweller did not cling to old-fashioned methods. Communications between management and workforce were excellent – the company assured people that policy changes would not result in job losses while trade union representatives were kept informed of all proposed innovations and were trusted to keep

their members up to date. 'Results are good, and, instead of mistrust, there is cooperation for the management through the understanding of new developments to meet public demand for their products.'[41] There were very few strikes, one of them taking place in 1973 out of sympathy with other trade unions during the turmoil created by industrial employment legislation.

41 Translation, Neue Zürcher Zeitung, 12 November 1961.

For Richard Walker, a good working environment was essential for getting the best out of people. That was one reason why so many people gave the company the best part of their working lives. This commitment, recognised for many years through the award of long-service bonuses, was marked in 1961 by the creation of the 21 Club for every employee who had achieved 21 or more years with the business. Another step forward came in 1964 when the company extended its life assurance and pension scheme to cover every employee over the age of 30 with more than five years' service and made the scheme non-contributory.

Physical expansion was still possible on the Cheltenham site although space was becoming more cramped. In 1964, with sales, exports and profits up, the company raised more capital to fund a 10,000-sq.-ft extension. Completed in 1965, this comprised a tooling shop, drawing office and work study department and freed space for much needed extra production capacity. Around the same time, a new building was completed for the research and development team, which incorporated the largest hydraulics laboratories in Europe, capable of reproducing water supply conditions from anywhere in the world. The new canteen catered for a burgeoning workforce, which totalled 700 people by 1970.

By then, there was little room left on the existing site for further development other than adding

The 21 Club,
July 1967.

Walker's Europe mixture

RAPIDLY rising sales of its water mixing valves and taps in the Common Market are making Walker, Crosweller seriously consider setting up a new factory on the Continent. At the moment sales to the Six make up less than one-fifth of the group total, but within three years this business is expected to become more important than the UK division—which indicates a trebling of Continental sales by 1968. Last year orders from Germany and Belgium rose by 76 and 59 per cent. respectively and with this market becoming so important chairman Richard Walker is apprehensive of any increase in tariffs. Already Walker, Crosweller prices are about 20 per cent. above those of their German competitors—the company's success at the moment depends on better design and shorter delivery dates. In the year ended in March, group profits leapt by 80 per cent. and there should be another sizeable increase this year. Benefits of a large extension to its Cheltenham works were only felt in the last quarter of last year and delivery will be taken of new machinery in August which will give the company all the extra capacity it requires. The 5s. shares came back to 23s. last week following the results where they yield 4.3 per cent. covered more than three times.

Bryan Wharton

Richard Walker: a trebling of continental sales by 1968

floors to existing buildings, and the company was seriously considering another UK factory. Instead, to create space on site, several operations were relocated in 1973 to units on the industrial estate at Kingsditch Lane in Cheltenham. One, known as KL1, was occupied by the plastic injection moulding department; the other (KL2), by the Arkon machining and assembly operations, both managed by Roy Davis. He was one of many examples of long-serving employees being given the chance to

Richard Walker enthusiastically and successfully promoted the company's exports throughout the 1960s.

develop greater responsibilities. He had joined the company as a fitter in 1952, becoming chargehand and foreman, then assembly and finishing superintendent, before taking charge of the plastic moulding operation. The space vacated on the main Cheltenham site was used to construct the half-a-million-pound 40,000-sq.-ft Building 20. Begun during the short-lived boom of the early 1970s, it was completed in very different circumstances in 1974, as oil prices rocketed, inflation soared and industrial strife was commonplace.

The company was achieving record exports as well as record UK sales. In 1965 they accounted for a third of all sales and in 1968 Walker Crosweller was exporting to 80 countries worldwide. Europe – and West Germany in particular – was by far the most important export market. The West German subsidiary had been joined by another formed in Belgium in 1961, under the management of a

West Germany was an important market for the company and this newspaper cutting shows clients from Germany on a visit to Cheltenham in 1964.

Working in Exports in the 1960s

Roy Minett joined Walker Crosweller as an export shipping clerk in 1968. He remembered how he wasn't so much interviewed as sold the company by Rene Geissler, who opened Roy's eyes to the wider world of overseas business.

He recalled that the company playing field was still in use – it was built on in the early 1970s – for football and cricket and there were matches between departments. The layout of the canteen, he remembered, reflected the company's hierarchical structure; it was divided into three areas, one for the shopfloor (hard flooring), one for office staff (carpet tiles) and one for directors (waitress service).

The export department comprised a filing clerk; three export shipping clerks, each with an allocated typist; an office supervisor; an office manager; two overseas salesmen and an export sales director. Behind the export section, located on the second floor of the main building, was the typing pool of about a dozen young women. Every letter was either hand-written or dictated before it was sent for typing. Roy's desk consisted of pen, pencil, paper and a rotary dial telephone. Messages were sent overseas by telex, with the telex operator typing the message onto tape. Roy's job involved receiving overseas orders and liaising with other departments to establish the availability of products and spare parts. He chased orders, marshalled products, closed cartons and liaised with shipping agents. Exports were made up mainly of commercial products, using bimetallic technology, for sectors such as healthcare, sport and leisure, defence, and industry. The company also exported steam-and-water mixers, particularly to Japan.

former Belgian international footballer, Guy Dooms, which was also a platform for selling into France. A well-established network of agents promoted the company's sales in other markets. Senior executives travelled frequently overseas and the company continued to welcome representatives of its agents to Cheltenham.

New markets were always under consideration – the company exhibited at a trade fair in Zambia in 1965, for instance – but outside Europe Richard Walker was especially keen to make further inroads into North America. A third subsidiary was established in Canada in 1963 under resident director George Staff. In 1967 UK sales manager Brian Knight was sent out to set up a marketing organisation in New York, echoing the visit made to the city nearly sixty years earlier by Walter Crosweller.

Taking the chairman's first two names, the new company was called Richard Fife Inc. In 1967 the company appointed an agent in Japan, Toshio Shimada, of the Toyoshi Trading Co., Osaka, and by the early 1970s, Japan was the second largest importer of Leonard thermostatic mixing valves. Another subsidiary company was formed in South Africa in 1974.

Exports had been expected to outstrip UK sales by the mid-1960s, but the company was hindered in this objective by tariffs on UK exports to Europe, which made the company's products a fifth more expensive than those of its European rivals. The company remained competitive, it was claimed, thanks to more attractive design and shorter delivery dates. Understandably,

Richard Walker was an enthusiastic advocate of the UK's membership of the European Economic Community (EEC). Serious thought was given to setting up a factory in Europe, but the plan was put on ice as the cost of borrowing increased and never revived.

In 1973 the company achieved record sales, which exceeded £4.5 million, with exports accounting for a quarter as the UK joined the EEC. By then, however, the oil crisis was bringing an end to the almost uninterrupted continuous rapid growth enjoyed by the company during the previous decade. Roger Tallis recalled how the company strove to maintain full employment at a time of power shortages and the imposition of a three-day working week. This led, for example, to a sub-contract for the making of rotary selector valve bodies for Dowty Mining, which continued for several years. By the end of 1974, the company reported, sales were static, margins were squeezed and the completion of a four-year expansion programme, with the opening of Building 20, had resulted in overcapacity.

By then, Richard Walker was in his mid-60s. He had hoped that his son Sebastian would join the business. He had been expected to take up a position as a special assignment representative on 1 October 1970. An office was prepared for him, recalled Roy Minett, but he never turned up. Sebastian's sister Mirabel recalled that a less likely engineer than her brother was impossible to consider and although he did spend some time in the factory it never suited him. His father expected him to work his way up through the company on merit but Sebastian, writing to his father, insisted he would join only on the promise of becoming a director. In his reply, Richard stressed Sebastian should make up his own mind about his future career, 'and on this point you can – and I say this with complete sincerity – ignore my feelings … I applaud your ambition to make your own career'.[42] Instead, Sebastian became a publisher's sales representative, demonstrating a real flair. Recognising his son's potential, Richard Walker

Mixing Valves
LEONARD thermostatic mixing valve have an important application in the field of hydrotherapy. Temperature o pool sprays, which must not exceed 100° F, can be controlled automatic

Valve controls spray temperature
ally by these valves. Leonard valve can also be used in the control o showers and footsprays.

introduced him to his own bank, which lent him the money to start his own publishing business. Founded in 1978, and specialising in children's literature, Walker Books became hugely successful.

Without family succession, Richard Walker had to consider the future of the business once he retired. A suitor was sought and in 1975 Walker Crosweller became part of industrial conglomerate Reed International.

42 Sebastian Walker 1942–91: A Kind of Prospero, Mirabel Cecil, London, 1995, p48.

4 Changing Ownership: 1975–2001

The agreed bid from Reed International in the spring of 1975 was worth £2.4 million, with Reed paying a premium of more than 50 per cent on the value of the shares. Reed already owned other similar businesses, including sanitaryware manufacturer Twyford, and believed Walker Crosweller would complement its building materials division. Richard Walker remained chairman until his retirement in 1979 when he was succeeded by the chief executive of Reed Building Products, Michael Collins. Following the takeover, he handed over as managing director to Dennis Arbon, who had been director of research and development. This appointment gave continuity but it was also a sign that Reed was happy for one of the most successful businesses within the building products division to carry on doing its own thing. Reed International turned out to be a beneficent parent, standing back with a watchful eye while continuing to nurture the business through continuing investment.

There were other senior management changes as others of Richard Walker's generation, like A L Hancock and C F Taylor, retired. Under Dennis Arbon, Ron Harrison continued as works director with Jim Harrison as marketing director and Mick Brooks as general manager.

Domestic showers were becoming more popular, helping the company to recover from the recession of the first half of the 1970s. Alan Schuman, the Mira general sales manager, told the press in 1977 that 'over a decade or two, the bathtub could be entirely replaced'.[43]

One of the trends concerning the company was the rising popularity of electric showers, which accounted for more than half the £50 million UK shower market in 1976. This was a worry since Walker Crosweller did not make a single electric shower. Initially, the company decided to counter this development by strengthening the marketing of its existing range of showers. Advertising emphasised the Mira's advantages – cheaper to run, cheaper to install, more reliable, with a better flow rate. New packaging, promotion and branding all paid off, generating demand that outpaced production, with lengthening deliveries, resulting in night-shift working to cut the backlog. Every product was rebranded under the Mira name; the first Mira thermostatic shower, the Mira 722, was a close derivative of the Leonard 72. The benefits of the thermostatic shower were

43 Birmingham Daily Post, 9 Feb 1977.

Working on the Night Shift

Nina Prajapat's family came to the UK from Kenya in 1968. Originally, she settled with her husband in London, but then in 1977 his job was moved to Cheltenham. She wanted part-time work as she had a two-year-old son but didn't know where to look. One day in the local park she was talking to a woman who said Walker Crosweller was recruiting part-time workers. She rang the company and Derrick Peacey invited her to an interview, telling her she could bring her young son along. 'That was so nice of him!' While being interviewed, her son was able to play on the computer, and when she was shown around the machine shop, although children shouldn't have been allowed in, he was carried around on the shoulders of the maintenance man. Nina worked on the 4.30 p.m. to 10 p.m. shift with lots of other women who found part-time work ideal. Doug Green, ex-army, very strict, was in charge of the shop, which milled and drilled covers for various shower models. It was oily and noisy, and ear plugs were handed out, which was about the limit of health and safety precautions. On piece-work, she was turning out 200 items an hour. After some time, she asked why she wasn't being offered any other type of work, and was told it was because she was the only operator who didn't cause the AN2 machine she was working on to break down. She did eventually move around other jobs but was always the favoured No. 2 operator for the AN2. In the machine shop, Gerry Finnegan and Derek Preston were always helpful when there was a problem, as were other girls finishing their jobs early.

73

becoming more obvious. Installers liked it since it was much more tolerant in instances where it was impossible to balance cold and hot water pressures within a household system, while, once installed, consumers appreciated the advantages of thermostatic control.

All this gave Walker Crosweller the breathing space to develop its first electric shower, launched under the Miralec name in 1978. Initially, the company's advertising was almost apologetic.

An advertisement placed in a Sunday newspaper highlighted at length the advantages of Mira thermostatic mixer showers before adding almost as an afterthought in conclusion: 'You might expect Mira to be biased against electric showers. After all, we are the leaders in the mixer shower field. There is a simple answer: Mira also sell Miralec showers … For some people, the electric shower is best … but for most of us, the Mira mixer type is the most luxurious and most economical shower one can

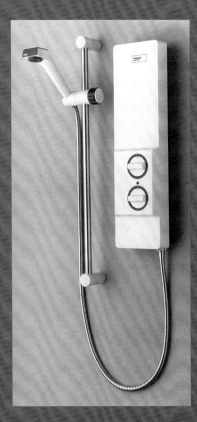

The Miralec Supreme was the first Mira-designed electric shower. The brand was first launched in 1978.

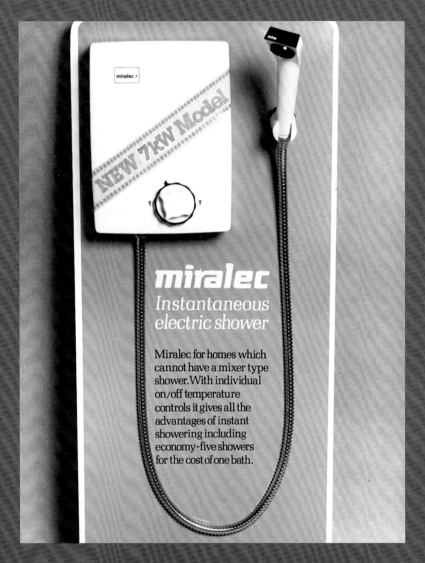

miralec
Instantaneous electric shower

Miralec for homes which cannot have a mixer type shower. With individual on/off temperature controls it gives all the advantages of instant showering including economy-five showers for the cost of one bath.

The Miralec 7 electric shower followed the Miralec Supreme, its boxy shape more like many later electric shower designs.

The plastic moulding department based at Kingsditch Lane in Cheltenham.

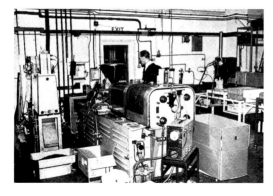

buy.'[44] As electric showers became more popular – today the company sells over 400,000 every year – they were added to the Mira range and the Miralec name was dropped.

Pete Green recalled working with Bob Meadows on the new electric showers. As with the first Mira shower, the first electric shower was sourced from an external supplier, in this case, the

44 Sunday Mirror, 19 August 1979.

electrical engineering manufacturers IMI Santon. The first electric shower developed entirely by Walker Crosweller was the Mira 7, the numeral denoting the kilowatt power of the heating element. This gave the company a foothold in both sides of the domestic shower market: plumbed-in mixer showers and cheaper-to-install electric showers. The space devoted to electric shower manufacture in the Cheltenham factory soon became inadequate and in 1981 production was transferred under the management of Derek Preston to Kingsditch Lane.

Around the same time, the company acquired from Drayton the Hydroflex business, which mainly produced hydraulically formed metal bellows. The business was housed in unit KL1 on the Kingsditch Lane estate. The bellows were central to the thermoscopic technology the company was developing under Roy North as the principal designer. Dennis Arbon came up with the name, conflating thermostat and telescopic (the movement made by the valve). Traditionally, thermostatic mixing valves had employed a coiled bimetallic strip, which was quick to respond to changes in temperature. The disadvantage was that the performance of these strips deteriorated over time with the build-up of limescale. Moreover, they were becoming more expensive to produce. Thermoscopic products were superior in several respects as Roy Minett later described them to a trade journal. The first iteration of this

75

Families and Friends

The sports and social club remained a focal point for employees during the 1970s. There were skittles competitions and discos and outings to places such as Weston-super-Mare and Alton Towers. At Christmastime, there were parties and pantomime trips for employees' children as well as the Christmas dance for the adults, often held at the Racecourse. There was also a popular gardening club. As part of Reed International, the football club took part in the Chairman's Soccer Trophy competition. The list of long-serving employees grew longer, with several completing more than 40 years with the business, including Richard Walker and Derrick Launchbury. There were frequent gold watch presentations to people achieving 25 years of service. Family relationships were strong – in 1979, for instance, the company recorded 53 relationships, covering 108 people, who were brothers and brothers-in-law, fathers and sons, husbands and wives, brothers and sisters, aunts and nephews. For instance, Don Newman had recently retired after 39 years, his daughter Eileen Harper had completed 24 years and his grandson Colin was employed as a storekeeper. New blood continued to flow into the company through the apprenticeship scheme and by 1979 38 apprentices were in training.

technology comprised, he said, 'a bellows device with a long copper capillary tube, within which we incorporated a thermoscopic compound that changed from a honey-like state into a liquid as the temperature rose. The material was also highly corrosion-resistant.'[45]

The small metal bellows were supplied by Drayton Controls, which many years earlier had supplied the original Arkon measuring instruments to Walker Crosweller. Shortly before the launch of the first thermoscopic products, the Rada 15 and Mira 915, in 1979, Drayton suddenly decided to close its bellows production. Walker Crosweller stepped in to take over the assets of the business, renaming it Hydroflex. Developing the expertise needed to make the bellows was a challenge, but the business was bolstered by demand from other former customers of Drayton. The bellows were used, for instance, to monitor the oxygen supplies for jet fighter pilots. By the early 1990s, 80 per cent of Hydroflex business was for external customers.

The original innovative thermoscopic design won an award at the 1979 Batimat Building Exhibition held in Paris. An improved version was

45 Health Estate, January 2014.

introduced in 1984, which was less expensive and quicker to respond to changes in temperature, but the company concluded that there was little economic benefit in exploring further advances in mechanical thermoscopic technology. Instead, a more reliable wax-capsule system, supplied by French manufacturers, was used for thermostatic products, and the Hydroflex business was eventually sold off.

This was not an easy time for any manufacturing business in the UK. By the late 1970s, the country was plagued by industrial unrest; the strikes that took place during the winter of 1978–79 represented the largest stoppage of labour since the 1926 General Strike. The new Conservative government embarked on an economic strategy that brought down inflation but only at the cost of soaring unemployment, which reached 3.3 million, and a sharp decline in UK manufacturing.

Sending out the seasons' greetings to employees at Christmas 1978, Richard Walker stressed that the company must continue to produce innovative, well-designed, quality products which met the needs of the customer and were accompanied by good service and aftersales care. 'We build our business by creating customers,' he said. It was around these traditional strengths that Dennis Arbon and his team developed their strategy to tackle the recession. Their aim was to retain market leadership by continuing to invest in an improved

and extended range of products while driving down costs in other parts of the business.[46] For example, the plastic moulding operations at Kingsditch Lane were outsourced to another business within Reed International. The vacant unit was later taken over for assembling electric showers, doubling existing operating capacity. With low employee morale, every effort was made to minimise job losses through natural wastage, retirement and transfers. Under general manager Alf Wainwright, the research and engineering department maintained a steady stream of new products. As well as the thermoscopic range and the new electric showers, these included coin-operated showers, timed flow controls, emergency shower equipment and automatic electronic flow controls with infrared sensors.

At the same time, the company was reorganising its export operations, reverting to its original policy of trading through independent agents and distributors. In Canada, the USA, Switzerland and South Africa, the business was taken over by previous managers. The exception was in Europe, where existing subsidiaries were joined by a new company formed in France in 1975. The most important was still the West German company, which in 1979 had 13 representatives and 6 engineers under manager Harry Hesser.

46 Walker, Crosweller World, Christmas 1978.

Caradon Flag image outside site entrance, c.1980.

As the economy pulled out of recession, the company resumed investment in other areas of the business, and results began to improve once more. Investors, however, were falling out of love with diverse industrial conglomerates, like Reed International. In 1985, Reed reviewed its operations and concluded that its building products division was no longer an essential part of its business. This prompted the division's senior executives, including Dennis Arbon, to make a successful £61 million bid for the business, including Walker Crosweller. It was Dennis Arbon who provided a new name, Caradon, for the business, taking it from the area of his beloved Cornwall where he had a house. He remained managing director of Walker Crosweller, which also changed its name to become Caradon Mira, reflecting the growing recognition of its leading brand. A mild-mannered man, approachable, open and pragmatic, he was an enthusiastic exponent of the business, which was regarded as the jewel in Caradon's crown. With his strong commitment to research and development, he was always urging people to keep innovating.

The Foundry

For many years this was an integral part of the factory until production was outsourced in the late 2000s. Andy Bearman was 19 when he started work in the foundry in 1987. He began by making castings for the valves of showers like the 915. It was hot, noisy and dirty. Sometimes molten metal that was poured into the high-pressure diecasting machine flashed out of the dies and covered you in a fine dust. But the company, Andy recalled, had a good reputation for health and safety under health and safety officer Jack Keeble.

Dennis Arbon stepped down as managing director in 1987, when Caradon became a public company, raising £134 million. Its independence was short-lived. In 1989 it became part of the industrial group Metal Box for £338 million. Metal Box, which soon changed its name to MB Group, had undergone a recent revival after a significant restructuring and had interests in several related businesses, including Stelrad and Doulton. The merged business became known as MB-Caradon. Bob Winstone succeeded Dennis Arbon as Mira's managing director.

Prior to the merger with Metal Box, the most significant developments within Caradon Mira were the lease of the distribution centre at

Meynell Valves

Based in Wolverhampton, Meynell was founded in 1798 as an agricultural engineering business, later making gas fittings as well as cast-iron fountains for country estates. It made firefighting equipment during the Boer War, pumps and valves during the First World War and taps for the water carts used by the Eighth Army during the Second World War. It was variously described as non-ferrous founders and engineers (1952) and fluid control specialists (1958), only later specialising in mechanical and thermostatic mixing valves. After its acquisition by Caradon in 1988, it continued to be run separately until a decision was made to integrate the business within the Cheltenham factory, completed in 1997.

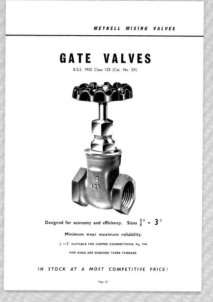

Meynell Valves, Wolverhampton, was founded in 1798 and became part of Caradon in 1988.

Apprentice Memories:
Adrian Coleman and Haydn Cooling

Adrian Coleman and Haydn Cooling both joined Mira as apprentices after leaving school, Adrian in 1989 and Haydn in 1990.

Adrian began his training under Derrick Peacey at the onsite training centre, which was refurbished soon after Adrian started. Apprenticeships lasted four years, and Adrian was one of five new Mira apprentices, along with half a dozen apprentices from other local engineering firms who came for their first year's training. 'We were really lucky because the training was fantastic.' The first year, comprising basic engineering skills, was 'robust and challenging', and only three Mira apprentices completed it, including Adrian.

When he started, Adrian was paid £73.50 a week, which he thought was great for a 16-year-old still living at home. 'A lady came round every week pushing the wages trolley, handing out brown envelopes full of cash: what more could you want?' By the time Haydn Cooling joined, pay slips had replaced cash, but the trolley still came round. He remembered how the finance department was used as a bank on pay day, with employees writing out cheques for cash at the cash office's small hatch.

In the second and third years, the training differed for technical and craft apprentices: the former spending more time in technical areas, the latter more time on the shopfloor.

In year four, apprentices focused on their chosen area in preparation for the job they were almost certainly guaranteed to get at the end of the year. In Adrian's case, he was assigned to the customer service director, who had a project involving the replacement of a specific model from a number of retail stores in the UK. Adrian travelled from store to store, swapping old for new stock. The director was so impressed he suggested he should become a service engineer. At the age of 20, Adrian spent eight months learning on the job with a senior engineer, getting to know a limited product range, and enjoying being out on the road and using his skills. 'You could not have had any better training.'

Haydn spent his fourth year in purchasing. Everything was still done manually. So, in an era before the PC, every report or enquiry was written out, collected by the post lady, Dot Yates (whose husband Bob was head security guard), and sent to the typing pool before being returned for correction. It could take days for a letter to be sent out. Smoking was still permitted – by mid-morning smoke hung in a haze across the customer service office. Non-smokers worked alongside people smoking cigarettes, cigars and pipes.

Adrian was active in the Apprentice Association, first as treasurer, then in his fourth year as chairman. The canoeing test was then run by the Young Gloucestershire youth organisation. Participants pitched camp every night and the following day completed 25 miles in their canoes before returning to camp.

Both Adrian and Haydn recalled the 'jailbreak' when groups dressed in boiler suits marked with old-fashioned prison arrows were challenged with getting as far away as possible from Gloucester prison in 12 hours.

Adrian's group succeeded in hitchhiking to Dunblane – they didn't win because another group got to France – where they persuaded one hotel to give them food and a room free of charge for the night. The next challenge was getting back to Cheltenham on a Sunday to make sure they were back in work for Monday morning. They were fortunate that within half an hour they were picked up by the driver of a BMW 3 series estate, who had been up to Scotland for a shooting weekend. He told them he was heading for Bristol and dropped them all off in Cheltenham.

Haydn took part in two jailbreaks; on the first, his group reached Lockerbie; on the second, Glasgow. In Lockerbie, this group of teenage boys spent the night at the local disco; in Glasgow, they managed to persuade a hotel to give them a room free for the night (discovering the minibar was stocked only with soft drinks).

Barnwood, near Gloucester – another move that freed up more space on the Cheltenham site – and the acquisition of Meynell Valves in 1988 to expand machining capacity.

One of the benefits of belonging to MB-Caradon was continued support for personal training and development. This was now an all-embracing topic, with an impact on every part of the business. In 1989 the theme was better product design and quality, delivery and aftersales service; in 1991, as another economic downturn hit the construction industry particularly badly, creating more competition, the emphasis was on improving manufacturing quality through the adoption of production cells and better team working. The first production cell was formed in July 1991 with dramatic effects – the manufacturing cycle was cut from between three and four weeks to three days; the percentage of rejects was reduced to less than 1 per cent; there was a 5 per cent rise in productivity; stock levels fell by half; and there was an overall cost saving of 20 per cent.

But the initiative most remembered by those who took part was 'First in Service'. Launched in 1993, as the company's annual turnover exceeded £50 million for the first time, this ran for four years. Based on the concept of Total Quality Management, it encompassed the entire business, and aimed to instil within every employee an instinctive concern for quality and service. Haydn Cooling recalled how it helped to break down the silo mentality common in many factories in favour of more collaborative multi-functional teams. 'We very quickly learned we were working in an antiquated way,' remembered Martin Bull. Costly mistakes arising from batch production and working in silos were replaced by one-piece flow-working and an ethos of continuous improvement, which minimised errors and reduced work in progress. People began to deal with each other as customers rather than competitors. Phil Staelens was managing unit KL3 where shower fittings, handsets, hoses and power products were assembled, and recalled how the programme 'had quite a dramatic effect on people's working lives', creating a more relaxed working environment (jackets and ties were replaced by polo shirts) and boosting morale.

The expansion of training was one reason for the transfer of the apprentice training centre to the Gloucester College of Arts and Technology (GLOSCAT) in 1997. The former training centre was turned into a suite of rooms for all-purpose training. Another reason, however, was the centralisation of a lot of training at the new group plumbing and heating training centre at the Caradon Bathrooms site in Alsager, near Stoke-on-Trent. This filled a gap in the training offered to service engineers, allowing them to enjoy practical instruction on a range of the company's products. Christian Wagner was responsible for training engineers at the time and played a significant role in modernising the company's training approach. One of his innovations was the introduction of training videos and he ensured that the company kept up to date with changing technology, later using digital cameras and powerful laptops to create animated training presentations. His skills were utilised by the marketing department and he gave presentations on the company's products to audiences of plumbers around the country.

Mira sustained its high standard of apprenticeship training and continued to support people in furthering their qualifications beyond their initial instruction. Wayne Walker, for instance, who joined the company at the age of 16 after completing his 'O' levels in 1987, followed up his three-year apprenticeship, which included achieving his HND, with a degree in manufacturing systems at the University of Warwick. Two years after returning to the business, he took a master's degree in manufacturing leadership at Cambridge University. Another example is Jon Ramsdale, who joined as a graduate design engineer in 1996 and went on to achieve a number of additional qualifications, including two master's degrees. Today, Wayne is Vice-President Manufacturing Systems & Process Technology, and Jon is Operations Director for Kohler Mira.

The Apprentice Association remained active. In 1993, for instance, six members took part in bungee jumping, a team came second in the

national small-bore rifle shooting championships, a group of four took part in the traditional canoe test on the Trent and two teams entered rafts for a race on the Wye.

There was still a tradition among managers of taking a real interest in the career progression of younger employees. Nigel Breddy, who joined the export department in a clerical role in 1986, took a telephone call a couple of years later from Geoff Sandilands, who ran production control. Geoff invited him to come and discuss his future. 'Geoff was my first mentor, he made me think about what I wanted from my career, that there was more to life than going to the pub and playing rugby, and I have a lot to thank him for.' From production control, Nigel moved into sales, eventually becoming sales director. He was helped by many people along the way who had taken a positive interest in developing his career. Mira, he said, 'breeds opportunities for people who really want them'.

The company sustained its traditional commitment to research and development. The experimental department, where prototypes were developed, was refurbished, expanded and equipped with modern machines. The limited domestic product range – the commercial Rada brand boasted a bigger range than Mira – was improved and expanded. The first completely new product delivered during this period was the innovative Mira Excel mixer shower in 1990, which quickly became a best-seller.

At the time, Mira sold only two electric showers, the Mira M and the Mira Supreme, both with very low kilowatt ratings, although this would soon change, enabling more powerful showers. The Mira M was relaunched in an improved version as the Mira Sport in the late 1980s. It gained a reputation as 'the installer's favourite shower' because it was easy to install and reliable in performance. The Mira Elite in 1994 was a high-performance all-in-one electric shower designed for use where mains pressure was low and aimed primarily at the Irish market. The first completely new electric shower was the Advance in 1995, which was advertised as the world's first thermostatic electric shower and came in two higher kilowatt ratings.

The company had developed a couple of power showers, the Mira PowerRail and the Mira Express, but they were elementary and noisy. The PowerRail, for example, was essentially a wall-mounted pump linking a hose from an existing mixer shower to the shower head. Their replacement was the Mira Event. Introduced in 1993, in both mechanical and thermostatic versions, it was a pumped all-in-one mixer shower in thermostatic and non-thermostatic versions. Promoted as giving a gentler shower, it was less than half as noisy as competing products. By 1997, Mira had a 50 per cent share of the UK power shower market.

Another step along the road towards offering a complete shower package was Mira's relation with another Caradon group company called Alstone.

The Mira Excel launch team.

Founded in Hull in 1983, Alstone made shower trays and enclosures. But it was an underperforming business, hindered principally by inadequate premises. Plans were made to revive the business by investing in a new factory, but these would only reach fruition in the new millennium.

The sales organisation was overhauled to take account of the growing consumer market, and a national retail sales force was established in 1994. Two years later the first Mira Showers website was set up. Changes were emerging in the market as the big DIY retail shed operators, like B&Q, challenged the dominance of the traditional builders' merchants. Mira made its first breakthrough in 1999–2000 when the Essentials electric shower range was developed for B&Q. It was the first time the company had outsourced any manufacturing beyond the UK, a trend that would continue over the next few years as the Cheltenham factory gradually became a design-assembly-and-test facility.

Mira Excel

Developing the Mira Excel, launched in 1990, was challenging, groundbreaking and innovative. It was the first shower not to comprise brass internal parts. Instead of the traditional bimetallic coil, it was equipped with a plastic cartridge, making it more resistant to limescale and enabling the extension of the warranty from two to three years. It was the first model to be put through air testing rather than water testing and the first modern product to be branded with a name rather than a number. It was simple to install, with the highest flow rate of any mixer shower, separate easy-to-use controls for temperature selection and spray force and an easily set temperature regulator. A revised version was introduced in 2002. Craig Baker, later the company's managing director, led the 30-strong development team and still retains the model of the valve which was made in clear Perspex to help the team understand how it worked. 'It is probably the product I feel most proud of.' It remains Mira's most profitable product and was the UK's No. 1 mixer for many years.

MIRA EXCELS AGAIN!

The Mira Excel accounts for a massive 10% of the UK shower market value and in October this year it just got better!

Two extremely intensive development years and a massive amount of team effort have produced a range of products, which reaffirms our position as the number one shower manufacturers in the UK. Not only have we successfully launched a hugely improved Mira Excel, this time it's got a stable mate, the Mira Fino.

Mixing Perfection
The mixing capability of the new products has been a prime focus for the Orion Design team. To gain a greater understanding of how the water behaves inside of a mixing valve we employed a new CAD tool called CFD (Computational Fluid Dynamics). Through months of computer simulation, testing, and validation, the result is a vastly improved thermal performance, which positions the new offerings in a league of their own. Of course with such a breakthrough, we have patents pending which will protect the design for the next 20 years!

Maximising performance
Ceramic technology is a development area that has provided the new products with a significant leading edge. The ranges incorporate a specific ceramic plate configuration, which provides a much smoother flow control and gives a life of over three times that of the previous model.

With improved ceramics, larger filters, higher-pressure containment, and intensive testing, we now offer an increased guarantee period of 5 years.

Something for the installer
Mira Excel and Fino can be fitted straight onto current installations without the need for any pipework adjustment. For new installations, the products now include templates allowing the plumber to install quickly and accurately. All built-in variants have new 'LeakSafe' body seals to protect the wall in any event of a leakage, another first for Mira.

It doesn't come easy
Delivering Orion (project name for Excel, Fino, and Verve) did not come easy due to its size, complexity, and demand for innovation. Despite being presented with difficult challenges in all areas of the business the achievements have been fantastic.

Just some of the project highlights being:
- 33 new product/finish variants
- 350+ new components
- 52 man years of tooling
- 5 new suppliers
- 2 new polishing robots
- 1 new Riello machining centre
- 4 new castings
- In-house laser etching
- Development of the video camera ceramic setting rig
- 10,000hrs+ of life testing
- Introduction of Satin Chrome finishes
- £2.9m of capital investment!!

Whether it be organising market research, creating stunning product aesthetics, managing customer stocks, delivering highly professional sales launches, manufacturing hundreds of prototypes, collating and inputting a mountain of SAP data, or approving parts in China, the team commitment to launching the new Excel and Fino products is without parallel.

The order book is in line with forecast with some lines being much higher than expected. Great efforts are being made to smooth out production issues although it has taken just six weeks for the assembly lines to exceed the production rates of the old product. A superb achievement.

Mira Spirit and Determination
With a new product introduction that is undoubtedly the largest ever undertaken by Mira, it is easy to see how the business continues to go from strength to strength. The ability, attitude, and above all desire demonstrated is a tribute to everyone involved.

Mira Excel

Mira Fino

The Operations Consumer Cell Teams and support

The NPI Design team including Craig Baker - Project Leader (the one wearing a tie)

Stuart Sallis with Excel in the Plating Department

Originally launched in 1990, the Mira Excel epitomised Mira's reputation for innovation.

Mira Advance

The Advance is one of Mira's most successful products. It was the first fully thermostatic electric shower. The first shipments took place in February 1995, the culmination, as with other product launches, of a joint effort by teams in research and development, industrial engineering, manufacturing engineering, quality assurance, assembly, marketing and goods inwards. To date, more than two million units have been sold, equivalent in value to somewhere between £150 million and £200 million, and it still sells thousands of units ever year.

The first specified order for the Advance was secured by Les McCormack. With existing experience in sales, he had joined Mira as a sales representative covering the south-west in 1994. 'I felt at home very quickly. It was everything I wanted it to be.' He was impressed with the 13-week induction course, which taught him the positive aspects of selling. His trainer was Nigel Breddy, with whom Les has had a long relationship, today as national sales manager reporting to Nigel as sales director.

When Les visited the Devon & Cornwall Housing Association, he took along a battery-operated sample of the Advance on a stand. The customer, however, considered the Advance too expensive and wanted the cheaper Supreme. Les pointed out all the Advance's advantages – it could be fitted without the need for rewiring; it was easier to operate with push-button rather than rotary controls; the mechanism limiting the maximum temperature was more reliable and flexible. He won the sale because the customer recognised the advantages of the new model over the old in terms of meeting the duty of care the association had towards its tenants.

Launched in 1995, the Mira Advance is one of Mira's most successful products.

Legendary Service:
Joan Scammell

When a long-service lunch was held in 1994 for employees with 40 or more years of service, one of the guests was Joan Scammell, who epitomised the company's long tradition of customer service and aftercare. When she retired in 1995 after nearly 44 years with Mira, the company magazine, *Cascade*, said that 'her service reputation has become legendary'. She had joined Walker Crosweller from grammar school in 1951 and after a spell in buying moved into sales, where she was given the freedom to develop her role to embrace selling spares, giving service advice and demonstrating showers to the trade and public. Haydn Cooling remembered her running the showroom in Building 20. Any customer who had a query about their shower, whether a plumber or a member of the public, could come and see her. They were delighted when she handed out free service packs, typical of the company's approach to customer care. While Mira today remains the 'fit and forget' brand for many installers, they also appreciate the continuing availability of spare parts for products often decades old and the excellent service they receive.

Joan Scammell was well known for her outstanding customer service and spent nearly 44 years with the company.

Mira was not alone among UK manufacturers in looking to China as an alternative source of supplies. While Essentials was launched as a discrete brand, it came with a strapline stating it used Mira technology. The product was designed, tooled and supplied in nine months, and by the summer of 2000 it was available in 300 B&Q stores. Many people were involved in the project, including Craig Baker, later Mira's managing director, and Jon Ramsdale, later Mira's Operations Director.

Overseas, Rada became the umbrella brand for consumer and trade sales. By the late 1990s, the European market was still strong, as were sales to Japan, but the number of countries the company was selling to had dropped to 28. Rada products, which remained the company's UK commercial brand, underwent improvements during the 1990s. In 1990, through the acquisition of a Dutch business, Meltronic, the Rada Meltronic range was developed, distinguished by electronic timed flow controls, operated by movement rather than touch, making its use more hygienic. In 1995 the Rada 215, 222 and Exact thermostatic mixing valves were launched, featuring what was described as the world's first 'sealed for life' thermostatic cartridge, employing patented 'Radatherm' technology. In 1996 came the UK's first thermostatic tap, the Rada Thermotap, and in 1998 the Rada Pulse Washroom Control System was introduced, with its handheld programmer, optimising washroom water usage.

Under MB-Caradon, there was some investment in manufacturing, with £2.3 million spent on new plant and equipment between 1989 and 1995. By then the machine shop was equipped with 23 CNC machines, with the last manual machine being replaced in that year. In 1997 the Cheltenham factory won the award for UK Best Engineering Factory; the judges commented that it was 'a solid exemplar of manufacturing excellence across a broad range of performance measures and initiatives', and highlighted the high degree of commitment and active participation from employees. Robots helped to increase productivity; by 2000, for example, there were five robotic machines in the polishing and plating plant.

Much of this progress took place under Bob Winstone, who was managing director from 1987 to 1994. By then, Mira had secured its position as one of the star performers within the group, which was now called Caradon plc. During the next six years, however, the company had no fewer than four more managing directors. This was symptomatic of a feeling of almost constant change engendered under Caradon, which itself went through troubled times in the mid-1990s. There was a feeling that investment in the business did not match the contribution it made to the group's profits. Some people felt that parts of the Cheltenham site were beginning to look run-down. There seemed to be constant pressure to trim costs. It did not go down well when one group director, a guest at prize-giving, remarked he had won an award as one of the most frequent flyers on board Concorde, the supersonic airliner with premium ticket prices operated by British Airways. 'All this did,' recalled Steve Gamble, who had joined the company as a Rada product manager in 1993, 'was reinforce how out of touch those guys were … our profits were paying for those flights.'

Under Caradon, the most significant change was the creation in 1998 of Caradon Plumbing Solutions (CPS), which brought together the Mira, Twyford, Stelrad and Ideal Boilers brands. Too much change was attempted too quickly. Sales and marketing functions were centralised, with many staff relocating from Cheltenham to Caradon Bathrooms at Alsager, where Twyford was based. The latter's influence was felt in a sales approach based not on quality, which Mira had always adopted, but on price. With sales teams focused on merchants, it was a system that duplicated effort and pitted teams against each other, undercutting margins as a result. 'Millions were thrown away because we were trying to beat ourselves,' said Steve Gamble. Customers were alienated, with some switching to other suppliers. Once again, Mira was a shining star in the midst of this gloom, remaining consistently profitable. But the company was drawing heavily on the bank of goodwill it had built up with customers over many years. Nigel Breddy, part of one sales team based in Alsager, remembered the priority was hitting targets at any cost without any thought for the longer term. 'We weren't the Mira family – the whole feeling around the company changed.' The enterprise was short-lived, lasting just a couple of years, as sales collapsed. It caused 'a lot of heartache, a lot of lost sales, a lot of lost customers,' recalled Roger Tallis. Les McCormack remembered the chaos that characterised the various attempts to rescue the venture: if you were called to a meeting at nine in the morning, you knew you would lose your job; if you were invited to the midday buffet lunch, your job was safe.

Partly because of this commercial disaster, Caradon decided to sell CPS. In October 2000, HSBC Private Equity bought it in a cash-deal for £442 million. Investment ground to a halt as the new owners prepared the individual businesses for sale. The only benefit was that the structure of the business returned to the way it had been prior to CPS with the sales and marketing team returning to Cheltenham. Sarah Sadler had just joined the company as its first finance apprentice. 'It was a very unsettling time … it felt like forever … we didn't pay people on time, we didn't invest, we weren't allowed to spend any money.' Authorised requisitions were required for almost every item of expenditure. 'All of the heart was squashed out of the business,' said Steve Gamble.

5 The Kohler Mira Vision: 2001 Onwards

A series of suitors filed through the Cheltenham factory when HSBC raised the 'For Sale' sign over Mira. One deputation came from the Kohler Co., the global kitchen and bathroom group based in Wisconsin, USA. Roy Minett was charged with making a presentation about Mira to Kohler's representatives, but he had scarcely started before Kohler's chairman, Herb Kohler, interrupted and took over from him; Herb knew everything about the company, its history and its products. He had been trying to buy the business for 40 years and had been turned down three times by Richard Walker. This was his opportunity. His love for the business was evident. So too was his long-term commitment to the business. Kohler's values chimed with Mira's values, many of which were still rooted in its origins as a family business. The two businesses shared a belief in good design, quality and reliability, reinvesting profits, and harnessing the potential of a stable and committed workforce.

These shared values were evident even before the announcement on 19 July that Kohler's bid had been successful; Kohler had insisted that every Mira employee was briefed before the news was given to the press. On the following day, Herb Kohler came back to Cheltenham where he made two presentations covering more than 350 staff before travelling to Wolverhampton to address other staff. One of them, Haydn Cooling, recalled how Kohler's chairman told everyone how excited he was about Mira's future. He concluded his address by summing up the mission of the business – 'to contribute a higher level of gracious living for those who are touched by our products and services'.[47] The company magazine, *Cascade*, recorded how he had spoken passionately without notes about the two businesses: 'Having waited so long to acquire us, he stated that he doesn't intend to sell us and sees Kohler as a long-term parent.'[48] 'We were delighted when Mr Kohler came along,' said Nigel Breddy, a sentiment echoed by many people in the business. For another employee, Nick Rust, Kohler's ownership brought 'wonderful stability'.

For Dave Hill, Mira's operations director at the time, Kohler's detailed interest in decision-making was a revelation after the Caradon and HSBC years. 'It was a shock that we had a parent company that was prepared to take a real interest in everything we were doing.' The scrutiny was intense, with

47 Ibid.
48 Cascade, October 2001.

mira SHOWERS   ◆ **Meynell**   **rada** CONTROLS   **hydroflex**   **ALSTONE**

Cascade

October 2001   Issue 52

Herbert V. Kohler Chairman, CEO and President

Mira joins the
KOHLER® Co.
family of businesses

On Thursday 19th July, it was announced that the Kohler Co. had entered into an agreement by which the Mira Showers business including Alstone, would become part of the Kohler Co. family of businesses. The sale was completed on Friday 27th July and we are now all part of Kohler Mira Ltd.

The change of ownership, from a private equity group to a long-term owner from the same industry, was immediately noticeable in the style of communication of the sale. Kohler insisted that all Mira staff were briefed before any press statement was released externally.

Secondly, Mr Herbert V. Kohler and his senior management team immediately came to the UK on Friday 20th July to address staff. He made two presentations at Cheltenham covering over 350 staff and then travelled to Wolverhampton to address staff based there, plus the sales force and a representative group from Alstone.

Mr Kohler is grandson of the founder and is now Chairman, CEO and President. He brought with him his wife Natalie Black, Senior Vice President and General Counsel, his son David Kohler, Group President -Kitchen & Bath, Jim Westdorp, Sector President Global Faucets and Tom Adler, Financial Controller Global Faucets.

Mira Showers is now part of Global Faucets, which is part of the Kitchen & Bath Group so Richard White reports to Jim Westdorp, who reports to David Kohler.

The style of Mr Kohler's address to staff was also notable. Speaking without notes he spoke with passion about the two businesses for over an hour at each presentation. He has admired Mira for over 30 years and was visibly moved by their success in making Mira part of the Kohler family! Having waited so long to acquire us he stated that he doesn't intend to sell us and sees Kohler as a long-term parent.

He went through the history, organisation and values of Kohler to highlight the similarities with Mira's values and their approach going forward. High quality standards and leading edge design and technology are key. A stable, involved workforce who make things happen was another principle. A fourth, notable principle is that Kohler constantly re-invest at least 90% of their net earnings back into their business. We must put forward growth opportunities to win these funds but clearly this was a very encouraging statement.

Finally, Mr Kohler summed up the mission, which is to contribute to a higher level of gracious living for those who are touched by our products and services.

On a lighter note Mr Kohler was asked whether we could all attend the US PGA golf championship in 2004 which is being held at their Kohler golfing resort, Whistling Straits. With a wry smile, he said "sure if you hit all your targets it's possible." It's already clear that they have big growth plans for the UK.

Herbert Kohler, Natalie Black, David Kohler and Jim Westdorp.

The Kohler and Mira management teams

Herbert V. Kohler

Next Issue: Winter 2001

Kohler Co.

Kohler's history dates to 1873 when an Austrian immigrant, John Michael Kohler, bought the Sheboygan Union Iron and Steel Foundry in Wisconsin, which made cast-iron and steel agricultural implements, castings for local furniture factories and ornamental cast-iron pieces. Ten years later, he advertised his first plumbing product, a hog trough that 'when furnished with four legs will serve as a bathtub'. A flair for innovative design became a characteristic of the business. In 1911, for instance, Kohler produced the one-piece bathtub with built-in apron and

in 1927 launched the first colour-coordinated bathroom suites. As an article in Mira's magazine put it, 'From that point on, Kohler plumbing products meant beautiful form as much as reliable function.' More recently, Kohler has developed the master suite concept, based on harmony of design, while its bathroom products have been designed to maximise the conservation of water. Today the business is still owned and managed by the family, and the Kohler name is a global brand. It operates across six continents, with 48 manufacturing locations and some 38,000 employees.

a flurry of face-to-face reviews as each side got to know the other. Kohler believed that taking a longer-term view required detailed knowledge of the business to give it proper support.

Given so many similarities in culture and ethos between the two businesses, the process of integration following acquisition went smoothly. Kohler's ownership put a spring into Mira's step. Backed by investment from Kohler, Mira carried out the biggest new product launch programme in its history. Improved versions of the best-selling Excel and Event showers were introduced alongside two new models, the Fino and the Verve. The company magazine detailed the resources invested in these developments – 33

new product/finish variants, more than 350 new components, 52 employee years of tooling, 5 new suppliers, 2 new polishing robots, 1 new £670,000 machining centre, 4 new castings, and over 10,000 testing hours. Totalling £3 million, this investment easily outstripped in one year the sum Caradon had spent on the business in six. While most of the processes involved were based in Cheltenham, Mira had worked once again with external suppliers in the Far East. Sales shot up from £85 million in 2001 to break through the £100 million barrier in 2003. To celebrate that landmark, David Kohler flew over with his team and addressed the entire workforce gathered in Cheltenham Town's stadium.

92

mira · Meynell · rada · hydroflex · ALSTONE

Cascade

MIRA ACHIEVES £100m

In June 2003 Mira achieved £100m turnover as a business in its previous twelve months trading. This is a fantastic achievement and was celebrated by most of our employees at Cheltenham Town Football Club with David Kohler, Laura Kohler, Jim Westdorp and John Farrelly in attendance from Kohler Co. The event also coincided with two years of ownership by Kohler.

The Company was formed in 1921 as Walker Crosweller Limited changing its name to Mira in 1986. It was not until the mid 1980's that £50m turnover was achieved and in 1995 £75m, so the rate of growth is accelerating. As Roger Wilson said at the celebration event, 'it hopefully will not be too long before we are celebrating £150m especially with the launch of Kohler Bathrooms earlier this year'.

The reason that Mira continues to successfully grow is that the foundations of the Company are rock solid. We have a proud heritage of being leaders to market with innovative products, our products have a reputation for good quality, our after sales service is second to none in the industry and we do not rest on our laurels - we strive to continuously improve whatever we do. These foundations supported by the investment afforded to us by Kohler will allow the business to continue to grow. However the main reason for the success of the business is the people who have worked and continue to work here.

Thank you to everyone for your continued support and dedication to the business. Without you nothing is possible.

Over the next few years, other new products included Mira's first digital shower, the Magna, and new versions of successful models like the Sport. Under the leadership of Nigel Sansum (Senior Programme Manager), Mira established itself as Kohler's centre of excellence for thermostatic mixers, exporting the technology around the globe. The Mira digital mixing technology, which appeared in 2005, was used in several Mira and Rada products. While Mira was a brilliant engineering business creating reliable products loved by the installer, Kohler brought a greater emphasis on the aesthetics of design for the benefit of the consumer. Every product underwent a design review with Kohler's chairman; Herb Kohler never hesitated to put his own personal

Left Mira celebrates a significant milestone – achieving £100m turnover.

Below Associates celebrate the production of the two millionth tray at their Hull factory.

stamp on them, often choosing the more radical, bolder option. This was an ethos that percolated down through Mira.

When Kohler acquired Mira, it had also taken over Alstone, the shower tray and enclosure business based in Hull. A year earlier, Alstone had at last moved into new premises with a better layout and new equipment, a boost to morale and productivity. Ian Battye, the site production manager, played a vital role in the project. The business was integrated within Kohler Mira as Kohler Mira Tray and Enclosure. In 2002 Mira launched the Vision and Vista shower enclosure ranges, followed two years later by the Flight shower tray. The big leap forward with the latter came in 2008 in response to the plastic-skinned shower trays made by rivals. The outcome was an improved tray, which

93

The Mira team was awarded the Queen's Award for Enterprise in 2019 for their innovative Airboost technology.

used a patented design to reduce its weight while retaining its strength and rigidity. The success of the Flight technology gave Kohler the confidence to support plans for a new £6 million automated factory in Hull, which opened in 2012. Among the products emerging from the new factory was the Mira Flight shower tray. This sold over two million units over the next five years and the Mira Flight Safe anti-slip product in the range achieved for the company the Queen's Award for Enterprise Innovation.

(Mira gained a second Queen's Award in 2019 for its Airboost technology, used in its bestselling Sport Max electric shower, which increases volume by as much as 30 per cent without using any more water.)

The Rada brand, which had lost some of its distinctiveness during the 1990s, regained its impetus after Kohler acquired the business. This resulted in a string of innovative products, many of them designed specifically for the healthcare sector. Among them were the UK's first all-in-one surgical basin tap and thermostatic mixing valve range, the Unatherm (2003); the first digital thermostatic mixing valve for commercial applications, the Sense (2005), featuring no-touch controls; the world's first digital recirculating water temperature control valve, the DRV80 (2008); and the world's first digital mixing valve specially designed for healthcare use, the Acu (2009). The DRV80 revived Rada's position in the US, which has become the company's leading

In 2011 a new £6 million factory for making shower trays was opened in Hull.

export market as a result, thanks to Kohler's support and investment. Today, Rada's biggest growth opportunity is in the USA with its patented Intelligent Care system, which reduces the risk of waterborne pathogens, such as legionella, while maintaining protection from scalding.

The service side of the business was transformed through the transition from service agents to an in-house field service team, achieved over three years from 2001. Building 20 was reorganised to create space for another production facility, completed in 2005, helped by moving out the visitor centre and showroom to new premises. New processes and methods, such as the Kaizen technique, were introduced to encourage greater collaboration, speed up

innovation and boost productivity, developing further the concept of continuous improvement, a feature of the business since the 1990s. Project Cartridge in 2008, for instance, embraced many of these approaches in devising an updated cartridge manufacturing facility capable of increased output. Imaginative use was made of existing space onsite.

Kohler was also influential in helping to further leadership development within the business through initiatives such as One Leadership, launched under managing director Jeff Mueller in 2008, with support from Laura Kohler, Senior Vice-President of HR, Stewardship and Sustainability. The apprenticeship programme was revived after a period of neglect. Its value in helping to build a

CHAPTER 5: THE KOHLER MIRA VISION

stable workforce was highlighted in 2010 when it
was pointed out that 64 former apprentices were
still working for the business.

Jeff Mueller was supported by a strong
senior management team, including Dave Hill,
operations director; Richard Hastings, the finance
director; Daniel Brohn, marketing director; and
Craig Baker, the new product development
director. It was as Dave Hill took over from Jeff
Mueller as managing director in 2009 that the first
signs of the global recession became apparent.
'It was a tough time to be managing director.'
But Kohler was supportive, changing its focus
from annual growth targets to maintaining market
share. For a profitable business, with healthy
margins, falling sales had a major effect on the
bottom line. There was aggressive cost reduction,
with recruitment halted, early retirements and job
transfers. But there was minimal reduction in new
product development since Kohler saw innovation
as key to maintaining market share and the
company's ultimate revival.

Mira emerged from the recession leaner,
more agile and well placed for the upturn. As
Craig Baker, who had taken over as marketing
director, put it in 2013, the company 'aimed to
develop a continuous stream of innovative and
groundbreaking products which are – crucially –
targeted at the needs of our end customers …
Innovation, together with design, quality and brand
are our key differentiators against global and low-

cost competitors.' His successor as new product development director, Andy Baines, reflected Kohler's design vision when he added that new products should feature 'great industrial design, for consumer-oriented appeal, married with the finest cutting-edge technical engineering skills'.[49]

At the same time, the company continued to develop its multi-pronged approach to sales and marketing, covering the trade, DIY stores and online retailers. The latter were beginning to make their

49 Ibid., Spring 2013.

market, creating more choice for consumers, and influencing changes in the way installers operated. Mira seized the opportunities presented by social media to promote the business, directing more marketing at consumers while devising specific packages to consolidate links with installers. Merchants remained the conduit for supplying commercial projects on behalf of the NHS, local authorities, housing associations and housebuilders.

Under Dave Hill's successor, Liz Hazeldene, who took over in 2014, Mira benefited from Kohler's continuing commitment to the business.

CHAPTER 5: THE KOHLER MIRA VISION

In an interview with a local magazine, she described Herb Kohler's personal interest in the business. 'He knows our business strategy, our market, our competitive set and looks at the business holistically. Fundamentally, he cares.'[50] For the same interview, she highlighted two of Mira's traditional strengths – innovation through research and development, and people. Mira, she said, was 'the global showering centre of excellence with 120 people working in new product development and we invest heavily here'. And it was Mira's people who were critical for its

success. Her priority, she said, was 'building a work environment where people get to be the best version of themselves. If we can achieve that, the money takes care of itself. If people are happy and want to come to work to deliver what we are all focused on, then guess what, it works.'

These two strands, innovative product development and a committed workforce, have continued to take the business forward during the last few years. New products, the fruits of investment in the latest technology, from further automation to 3D-printing, have included the compact Mira Minimal and the Activate digital shower, controlled remotely using a smartphone.

50 Cotswold Life, 21 Apr 2015.

Apprentice Memories:
the First Finance Apprentice

Sarah Sadler joined the company on 3 July 2001 after 'A' levels as Mira's first finance apprentice. The evening before she started, she had driven to the site to make sure she knew her way. When she turned up on her first morning, after leaving the security office, she strode across the yard, 'completely oblivious to lorries and forklift trucks and crates, hollered at by the security guards, yelling "Stick to the path! Stick to the path!"' The site, she said, was 'alive and buzzing'. The college course forming part of the first year of her apprenticeship was suddenly cancelled, so she decided to move straight on to the programme for her second year. Unlike other apprentices, she was given a full-time job, in charge of the cashbook and cash office. Seeing the mountain of cash ledgers, she couldn't believe that everything was still being done manually until shortly before she joined. Two days a week she worked in the cash office, where on payday she handed out cash from the office's small hatch in exchange for cheques from a queue of employees whose pay had only recently been moved from weekly to monthly. She also arranged foreign currency in the days before the implementation of the

euro for people travelling overseas; handled the petty cash box, issuing cash for spending on teas, coffees and stamps; and managed expenses. As the apprentice, she was also tasked with sorting out the hundreds of invoices received in the post every day into alphabetical order for processing. 'Almost everything I did then doesn't exist now.'

Over the last 20 years Sarah has enjoyed any number of different positions in the business. These opportunities, and the ability to shape individual career paths, have been crucial factors in why Sarah and others have stayed so long with the business. Her great mentor early on was Nicky Berry, inspiring and demanding, whose trust and respect employees wanted to earn: 'She gave me the confidence to go further.' Similarly, when Sarah decided she wanted to fill a vacant position with the European finance team, she was offered the job on the spot, having put herself forward for it in a conversation with Richard Hastings, with whom she had worked in Mira before his move to Europe. He 'has been the biggest support and mentor to me. He was willing to take a chance on me and support me.' Since 2018 Sarah has been Kohler Mira's finance director.

Mira were one of only a few manufacturers who were able to meet the stringent requirements for ventilator testing and assembly required during the height of the pandemic in 2020.

One of the ideas driving the development of the latest series of digital showers is sustainability, with the aim of creating the best showers while minimising energy use.

Mira has surmounted two recent challenges, the impact of the UK's decision to leave the European Union in 2016 and the impact of the COVID-19 pandemic since early 2020. It has proved its resilience as consumers have turned towards brands like Mira which represent durability and quality. Mira's leading market share, for instance, is now 4 per cent higher than it was before the pandemic began. This growth was recognised at the highest level within Kohler Co. when marketing director Emma Foster and sales director Nigel Breddy were awarded the coveted Chairman's Award by Herb Kohler in November 2021.

The crisis also further underlined the commitment of Mira's people, highlighted in the initiative taken by manufacturing director Jon Ramsdale to develop ventilators, a project that produced a model ready for clinical trials in rapid time before the government decided it was no longer necessary. 'It was,' said Jon, 'a classic example of seeing people at their best. Everyone gave their all to see how we could help the NHS.'

Today, under Craig Baker, who became managing director in 2019, Kohler Mira is the UK market leader, with a share of around 40 per cent.

Previous pages Mira's multi-million pound new distribution centre in Worcester, opened in 2021.

It has annual sales of some £160 million, with the lion's share accounted for by the Mira brand, a testament to its remarkable success since the 1960s. It employs around 750 people, of whom some 250 are production staff. Many of the production processes previously outsourced overseas have now been brought back to Cheltenham. 'The pursuit of showering perfection,' said Emma Foster, the company's marketing director, 'has always been something that drives this business. In fact, in the early to mid-2000s, we used Showering Perfection as our consumer strapline, with the intention of highlighting the meticulous detail that goes into our products to ensure we give the person standing under one of our showers the best possible experience. As the brand continues to evolve, and we strive to ensure we are relevant for years to come, we aim to continue that thread of innovation and sustain the same trustworthy, pioneering spirit for the next 100 years, always placing our customers and the planet at the heart of everything we do.' The latest tangible sign of the belief Kohler has in Mira is the major £26 million investment in Mira's new automated distribution centre outside Worcester.

Other evidence of the successful relationship between parent and subsidiary is easily found. Over the last 20 years Kohler's investment has transformed working conditions. The dark, dingy working environment, where people commonly smoked around machines and used nothing but paper documents, has gone. People work in a bright and clean environment, where mundane operations are carried out by robots, and operatives are highly skilled, responsible for the quality of their own work, on which the reputation of the company relies.

It can be seen in the strengthening of ties with the local community, which has been an integral part of the business since Walker Crosweller first arrived in Cheltenham. The town can still call itself Cheltenham Spa partly because of help from Kohler Mira. In 2004, when Cheltenham's status as a spa town was threatened because of the declining mineral content of the water from the original borehole, the company sponsored a new borehole. Over the years the company has sponsored the shirts of the local football team, Cheltenham Town, while the south stand of Gloucester rugby club was renamed the Mira Showers Stand. Several of Cheltenham's many festivals have benefited from Mira's sponsorship, and the company's employees are encouraged to give back to the local community with each associate being given one day a year to volunteer for a charity.

All this helps to bring people together, from fundraising for charities (match-funded by the company), to events like Festival 100, held in September 2021 to mark the company's centenary, which attracted more than a thousand people, including past as well as present employees. The

Mira's sponsorship of Cheltenham Town
Football Club's FA Cup Fourth round draw
against Manchester City on 23 January 2021.

Mira's sponsorship of Cheltenham Town
Football Club's FA Cup Fourth round draw
against Manchester City on 23 January 2021.

21 Club, now renamed the Quarter Century Club, is still a forum for long-serving employees. (The value Kohler attaches to loyal service was obvious in 2004 when David Kohler, whose visit to the country coincided with the Club's annual dinner, took the opportunity to attend as a surprise guest, responding to the chairman's speech.)

What makes Mira a great place to work? For Roger Tallis, who retired in 2006 after 43 years, 'The work was always interesting. I had ten jobs and was involved for most of the time with innovation. All colleagues at the factory, we were all can-doers, we were always willing to give things a go.' 'It was the people, it really was the people,' said Nick Reichelt, who retired in 2016, 'followed by the products – and the technologies were great, and we were always striving to be ahead of the competition, with products all built to exacting standard. There was a great sense of belonging and that's why I stayed.' For Nigel Breddy, it is the strong team spirit that shines through the business – 'people like working with each other and enjoy each other's company'. 'I like coming to work', said Nick Rust. 'It feels like your extended family.'

In the company's centenary year, Craig Baker hands over a cheque for £105,000 to Elise Hoadley, Leckhampton Court Hospice Director at Sue Ryder.

David Kohler, President and CEO of Kohler Co.
officially opens the National Distribution Centre
in Worcester on 17 March 2022.

Current and former associates celebrate Mira's centenary at Festival 100 – a special event organised by the business.

'It has a family feel,' said Stuart Skinner. 'It's a nice place to work, people are driven and professional, they want you to succeed.' There is a pride in the business and its people. 'When you walk round the Mira plant,' said Wayne Walker, 'everyone welcomes you, and there is a genuine desire to share knowledge and information.' 'If you need help or advice,' said Kris Derrett, 'that's never an issue; it's a very open and forthcoming place.'

For Steve Gamble, 'they want you to grow and develop and they absolutely support you in doing that … they're extremely supportive in helping you to map out your career.' Craig Baker recalls how the company was always willing to give young managers more responsibility, echoing the ethos adopted by Richard Walker. He himself was just 31 when he was appointed new product development director. 'To this day, I remind myself

to be brave with young talent and give them a real stretch and push them on.' A great example of this is the recent promotion of Alex Fagg, himself a former graduate, to the role of new product development director. For Sarah Sadler, Mira's finance director, an outstanding example of successful promotion, continuing to give people the chance to develop their skills and careers beyond their own specialism remains crucial in attracting and retaining good people.

Today the business is more diverse, open and inclusive, thanks to the influence of Kohler's vision, which has raised people's awareness of the impact of their actions on those around them. Russell Harris, Customer Support Engineer Manager, stated that everyone's role is respected, and he praised the company's transparent management, the willingness to let people get on with their jobs and use their initiative, the receptiveness to new ideas and the understanding that not all of them would succeed. Mira has grown through strong leadership, a dedicated team ethos, the development of in-house talent and the ability to attract external talent. The strength of the brand is based on longevity, quality and innovation. The priority given to people percolates through to standards of customer service and aftercare. While the business has long recognised the value of fresh ideas from outside when appropriate, the company's tradition of long service brings

continuity, stability, familiarity and respect. Many of these qualities have been company traditions since its earliest days, and its continued success owes much to the ability of successive generations to refresh them and make them relevant for changing times.

On 25 January 2022, the business had the honour of welcoming Her Royal Highness The Princess Royal who learnt at first-hand about the values that have been at the heart of the business for over 100 years. During her visit, she toured the production facility and spoke to several associates representing different groups from the business. Among them were those who played an integral part in the production of ventilators

Princess Anne unveils a plaque marking the official opening of Mira's new innovation space, Space 100.

throughout the COVID-19 pandemic as well as representatives of the charity fundraising team. The Princess spoke warmly of Mira's 100-year long history, specifically highlighting its innovation and its commitment to sustainability before unveiling a commemorative plaque to mark the occasion. In reflecting on the company's milestone anniversary, David Kohler, President and Chief Executive

of Kohler Co., remarked that 'Mira has been a fantastic acquisition for us. For the last 20 years the business has delivered some industry-leading results and provided both showering innovation and talent to the wider Kohler organization. On behalf of all Kohler associates around the world, I would like to congratulate the team on their centenary. Here's to the next 100 years!'

Acknowledgements

114

It has been a pleasure putting together this short history of Kohler Mira and it could not have been achieved without the willing help of so many people in the company. I would especially like to thank all those who agreed to be interviewed for the project, contributed written reminiscences and helped to answer queries: Jim Amphlet, Craig Baker, Andy Bearman, Nigel Breddy, Martin Bull, Adrian Coleman, Haydn Cooling, Kris Derrett, Roger Emmet, Emma Foster, Steve Gamble, Pete Green, Dave Gregory, Russell Harris, Dave Hill, Les McCormack, Roy Minett, Nina Prajapat, Jon Ramsdale, Nick Reichelt, Nick Rust, Sarah Sadler, Stuart Skinner, Roger Tallis, Christian Wagner and Wayne Walker. I would like to thank Craig Baker for his support throughout the project and Elisa Paratore for all her help from its inception. As the story of Kohler Mira demonstrates, collaboration and cooperation are at the heart of its success, and I have had the privilege of seeing those qualities first-hand. If, in spite of all this help, any errors remain, then they are mine alone.

Nigel Watson

Timeline

Date	Event
1879	Birth of James Macfarlane Walker
1888	Birth of Walter Crosweller
1911	Walter Crosweller joins Sanders, Rehders & Co., the predecessor of Spirax-Sarco, and takes over New York office
1913	First thermostatic mixing valve (Leonard, USA)
1914	Sanders, Rehders & Co. design own first steam traps
1921	Walker, Crosweller & Co. formed in London
1926	Firm begins manufacturing in London
1926	Firm becomes sales agent for Spirax traps in the UK
1930	Firm incorporated as limited liability company
1932	Company takes stake in Spirax Manufacturing Company Ltd to begin making Spirax traps in the UK
1933	Company launches Arkon Instruments
1936	Company first imports Leonard mixing valves and secures distribution rights for most of the world
1937	Company relocates to Cheltenham
1938	Works social club formed
1939	Company sells its stake in Spirax Manufacturing Co. and its Spirax sales agency
1943	Walter Crosweller retired
1945	Company persuades the Ministry of Education to specify temperature-controlled washing facilities in new schools

Date	Event
1948	Company's export drive leads to branches in Zurich and Montreal
1949	Worldwide success of new thermostatic valve
1950	Company is the world's leading mixing valve producer
1950	Death of Walter Crosweller
1950	Factory extension planned
1950	190 employees and 2 UK branches and 2 overseas branches
1950	Leonard valves supplied to UK schools, hospitals and industry
1955	German branch formed
1955	Unatap patented
1956	Spray mixing taps range launched
1959	Leonard 72 valve – first mixing valve suitable for UK supply pressures
1961	Company goes public
1961	Advanced temperature controlled mixing valve launched
1961	21 Club formed for long-serving employees
1962	Advanced hydraulics testing facility opened
1963	Miraflo formed to market Mira 8 mechanical shower mixer made under licence from Denmark
1963	Richard Walker takes over as chair on his father's death
1964	National campaign to promote domestic showers
1964	Factory extension built
1964	Pension scheme extended to all employees and made non-contributory
1965	Mira 10 launched
1965	Arkon Manufacturing becomes Arkon Instruments
1965	Leonard 72 combined bath and shower control introduced
1966	Vacuum packing adopted
1966	The firm is the first in the UK to have airfreight cargo containers approved

Date	Event
1966	New research buildings, including the hydraulics lab, new apprentice training centre and new canteen
1966	Company set ups the Shower Information Bureau
1966	First computer installed
1967	Expansion into Asia: Japanese distributor appointed
1967	US subsidiary formed alongside export operations in Europe, Africa and North America
1968	Company advertises showers on UK TV for the first time
1971	Acoustic chamber installed
1973	Arkon and plastic moulding department move to Kingsditch Lane trading estate
1974	South African subsidiary formed
1974	Factory and office extension completed
1974	35 apprentices in training
1974	Mira 3 launched
1975	Walker Crosweller acquired by Reed International
1977	Experimental department moves out of its wooden shed
1978	Miralec electric shower launched and Leonard brand replaced by Mira Thermostatic
1978	Brian Knight buys out US subsidiary which becomes Lynwood USA
1979	Rada brand launched for export markets; Mira brand covers all UK products
1979	Award-winning thermoscopic mixing valves
1979	Richard Walker retired
1980	Miralec 7kW electric shower
1981	Thermoscopic electric shower launched for UK
1981	Rada 32RM is the world's first electronic mixer
1982	Factory production capacity doubled
1984	Mira first sponsors school students under the Engineering Education Scheme
1985	Launch of Mira electronic bathroom control system, integrating all bathroom electronic controls

Date	Event
1985	Buyout of Reed's Building Products Division creates Caradon
1986	Caradon Mira created
1988	Miralec becomes Mira
1988	Meynell, Wolverhampton, acquired
1989	Metal Box acquires Caradon
1989	Focus given to non-consumer products by creating International Technical Business Division
1990	Launch of Excel
1991	First MC production cell formed
1993	Mira Event launched
1994	National retail sales team formed
1994	Mira Elite launched
1995	The first thermostatic electric shower, the Mira Advance, is launched
1995	Rada Exact launched
1995	Hydrolab modernised
1995	Rada 215 and 222 (using Radatherm thermostatic cartridge technology) launched
1996	75th anniversary celebrated with family fun day
1996	First Mira website launched
1996	Rada Thermotap launched
1997	Apprentice training centre moved to GLOSCAT and suite of training rooms developed on site (1998)
1997	Factory wins UK Best Engineering Factory award
1998	Rada water usage control system launched
1998	Caradon Plumbing Solutions formed
1998	New Mira Sport range
1999	Reorganisation of manufacturing within Caradon Mira and Meynell through Project Flo

Date	Event
2000	HSBC buys Caradon Plumbing Solutions
2000	Richard Walker died
2000	Mira Essentials (3 series), Mira Design (7 Series) and Series 5 launched
2000	Alstone completes move to new premises in Hull
2001	Mira acquired by Kohler
2002	Mira enters trays and enclosures market
2002	Mira Excel re-launched
2002	Mira Event XS launched
2004	Company sponsors new spa borehole
2004	New visitor centre replaces former showroom and lecture theatre
2004	Move from service agents to field service team completed
2004	Mira Flight tray launched
2004	First Summer Bash
2005	First digital thermostatic mixing valve for commercial application launched under Rada brand
2008	First digital recirculating water temperature control valve
2011	New £6m shower tray factory opened in Hull
2012	Vision, Vier and Platinum Dual, Calibre, Agile and Adept launched
2017	Flight Safe tray wins Queen's Award (QA) for Enterprise Innovation
2019	Airboost water saving technology wins QA
2020	Dual outlet Electric Showers launched
2020	Mira takes part in Government ventilator challenge
2021	NDC wins BMA Carbon Reduction Award
2021	Shipments commence from new National Distribution Centre
2022	HRH The Princess Royal opens Space 100 to mark centenary
2022	David Kohler officially opens the National Distribution Centre

Index

122

1940

walker crosweller App...

surgeon's elbow
for use with leonard thermostatic m...

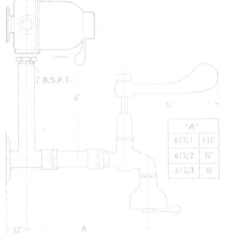

1" B.S.P.T.

6"

5½"

'A'	
612/1	11½"
612/2	7¼"
612/3	4½"

11"   A

Walker Crosweller and Company Limited

...r's Europe mixt...

...ales of its
...s and taps
...Market are
...Crosweller
...etting up a
...Continent.
...ales to the
...an one-fifth
...but within
...siness is ex-
...ore import-
...division—
...trebling of
...1968. Last
...ermany and
...and 59 per
...d with this
...important
...Walker is
...y increase
...ly Walker,
...re about 20
...se of their
...—the com-
...he moment
...design and
...es. In the
...ch, group

We devote in each edition
...age for
...KER CROSWELLER
...ICES ASSOCIATION

...iation was formed in
...has been gaining in
...very year. The Annual
...eeting was held recently
...next issue we will
...new officers for the
...

...biggest outside project

saves water
and water
heating costs

Leonard
72

thermos...
shower
combina...
& fitting...